CULTURALLY RESPONSIVE TEACHING IN MUSIC EDUCATION

Culturally Responsive Teaching in Music Education: From Understanding to Application, Second Edition, presents teaching methods that are responsive to how different culturally specific knowledge bases impact learning. It offers a pedagogy that recognizes the importance of including students' cultural references in all aspects of learning. Designed as a resource for teachers of undergraduate and graduate music education courses, the book provides examples in the context of music education, with theories presented in Part I and a review of teaching applications in Part II. *Culturally Responsive Teaching in Music Education* is an effort to answer the question: How can I teach music to my students in a way that is culturally responsive? This book serves several purposes, by:

- Providing practical examples of transferring theory into practice in music education.
- Illustrating culturally responsive pedagogy within the classroom.
- Demonstrating the connection of culturally responsive teaching to the school and larger community.

This Second Edition has been updated and revised to incorporate recent research on teaching music from a culturally responsive lens, new data on demographics, and scholarship on calls for change in the music curriculum. It also incorporates an array of new perspectives from music educators, administrators, and pre-service teachers—drawn from different geographic regions—while addressing the impact of the Covid-19 pandemic and the 2020 social justice protests.

Constance L. McKoy is Marion Stedman Covington Distinguished Professor and Director of Undergraduate Studies in Music, The University of North Carolina at Greensboro.

Vicki R. Lind is former Professor and Chair of the Music Department at the University of Arkansas at Little Rock.

CULTURALLY RESPONSIVE TEACHING IN MUSIC EDUCATION

From Understanding to Application

Second Edition

Constance L. McKoy and Vicki R. Lind

Routledge
Taylor & Francis Group

NEW YORK AND LONDON

Second edition published 2023
by Routledge
605 Third Avenue, New York, NY 10158

and by Routledge
4 Park Square, Milton Park, Abingdon, Oxon, OX14 4RN

Routledge is an imprint of the Taylor & Francis Group, an informa business

© 2023 Constance L. McKoy and Vicki R. Lind

First edition published by Routledge 2016

Library of Congress Cataloging-in-Publication Data
Names: McKoy, Constance L., 1956- author. | Lind, Vicki R., 1957- author.
Title: Culturally responsive teaching in music education : from
understanding to application / Constance L. McKoy, Vicki R. Lind.
Description: Second edition. | New York : Routledge, 2022. |
Includes bibliographical references and index.
Identifiers: LCCN 2022011358 (print) | LCCN 2022011359 (ebook) |
ISBN 9781032076539 (hardback) | ISBN 9781032076522 (paperback) |
ISBN 9781003208136 (ebook)
Subjects: LCSH: Music–Instruction and study. | Culturally relevant pedagogy.
Classification: LCC MT1 .L578 2022 (print) | LCC MT1 (ebook) |
DDC 780.71–dc23/eng/20220308
LC record available at https://lccn.loc.gov/2022011358
LC ebook record available at https://lccn.loc.gov/2022011359

ISBN: 978-1-032-07653-9 (hbk)
ISBN: 978-1-032-07652-2 (pbk)
ISBN: 978-1-003-20813-6 (ebk)

DOI: 10.4324/9781003208136

Typeset in Bembo
by Newgen Publishing UK

To the music educators who, over the past two years, have exhibited immense fortitude and commitment through the challenges of a worldwide pandemic and have navigated the difficult terrain of a national reckoning on race and equity. Because you have persisted, knowing how both events have significantly impacted students, we dedicate this second edition to you.

CONTENTS

PREFACE

A great deal has happened in the years since this book was first published. We have been so grateful for the support the first edition received, and we have witnessed a growing interest in culturally responsive teaching. We have had the opportunity to talk with teachers, administrators, and students across the country and we have witnessed some truly innovative approaches to music teaching that draw upon the expertise of diverse learners.

We have also observed a growing divide in this country and education has suffered as a result. In addition to attacks on critical race theory, as of this writing we are still living in the midst of a global pandemic. Our schools are operating during a time when the general population disagrees on how best to move forward. The pressure on teachers to adapt to an ever-changing model of instruction is unprecedented and we are increasingly hearing that parents, teachers, and students are exhausted. *On-line learning, hybrid classes, face-to-face classes, masks, social distancing, vaccine mandates…* these terms, some rarely used three years ago, now bring an immediate and emotional response regardless of one's personal and political views. Our schools are operating during an incredibly challenging time. So why are we writing a second edition now, under these circumstances? It is because we firmly believe that there has never been a more important time for us to critically examine how and what we teach.

Purpose of the Book

Culturally responsive pedagogy involves teaching in ways that are responsive to how different culturally specific knowledge bases impact learning. It is a pedagogy that recognizes the importance of including students' cultural references in all aspects of learning. Music educators are in a unique position to fully implement these practices in their classrooms given the intimate connection between music and culture. There has, however, been a disconnect in many classrooms between the music that is taught and the lives of the students and parents we serve. As we have visited with pre-service and in-service music teachers, and school administrators, we have heard many of them express a sincere desire to become more responsive, but they also described how difficult it can be. This textbook is written as a resource for all current and future music educators who are working to adopt a culturally responsive approach in their classroom.

We intend this book to serve several purposes. First, we want to provide a means for pre-service music teachers to understand the concepts of culturally responsive pedagogy from a music education context. We know that music education majors may be exposed to these concepts in their general education courses; however, transferring these understandings to instructional settings in music may be challenging. Additionally, while many aspects of culturally responsive pedagogy may be generalized across multiple academic subjects, some facets may have distinctive applications and functions for music education. We want to provide music education majors with examples of appropriate and effective implementation of culturally responsive pedagogy in music teaching and learning.

Second, we seek to translate culturally responsive pedagogy into a format usable for music education faculty in their undergraduate methods courses. Music education majors need opportunities to see how principles of culturally responsive pedagogy are applied in music education contexts and what culturally responsive teaching might look like in a variety of instructional settings in music.

Third, this text can be helpful to in-service music teachers interested in the topic of culturally responsive pedagogy and who would like to learn more about its application to music education practice. Music teachers who are seeking ways to make their teaching meaningful and effective for their students may find that a text focusing on culturally responsive pedagogy in music education can be a valuable instructional resource.

A fourth purpose is to make culturally responsive pedagogy accessible to music teacher education faculty and in-service music teachers by creating an accessible central resource. Through this text, music teachers and music teacher educators can introduce culturally responsive pedagogy into their respective classes and integrate it throughout their programs. Music teacher education faculty also can use the book to help identify in-service teachers who employ principles of culturally responsive pedagogy in their own teaching and who can serve as models for pre-service teachers.

What's New in this Edition

As with our previous edition, the title of our book reflects its organization. The first part of the book, *Understanding*, provides a foundation for comprehending culturally responsive pedagogy. Chapter 1 focuses on the nature of culture and the development of culturally responsive pedagogy in general education and in music education, along with a discussion of culturally sustaining pedagogy. Chapter 2 explores how culture informs the experiences and dispositions of teachers and includes updated educational data. Chapter 3 maintains the focus on how culture mediates child development and learning, and also provides new information regarding music preference and identity. Chapter 4 outlines the impact of culture on music learning as related to classroom, school, and community environments.

As before, Part II, *Application*, focuses on how the theories and principles presented in Part I are applied in classroom, school, and community contexts. How culturally responsive teaching informs instructional style and curriculum content is addressed primarily in Chapter 5. In Chapters 6 and 7, we discuss how school culture can foster or inhibit culturally responsive pedagogy, and how relationships between schools and the communities in which they are located can significantly influence possibilities for students' musical success. While we have continued our inclusion of teaching vignettes and suggested strategies, we have expanded the number and types of perspectives to include not only in-service, but pre-service music educators, and an educational administrator. These additions enhance the variety of settings which serve to contextualize the concepts and issues related to culturally responsive teaching presented in Part I. Chapter 8, "A Vision for Culturally Responsive Music Education," concludes Part II. As in our first edition, we offer a glimpse of what might be possible when music instruction is responsive to culture, and what that could mean for the future of music education in the United States.

How to Use this Book

Our focus on theory and application provides for flexibility in the approach to using the text in teaching. One could choose to delve deeply into the theories presented in Part I and follow with a review of teaching applications in Part II. Alternatively, one could focus primarily on Part II and reference the theory presented in Part I to frame discussions. The organization allows for the reader to move flexibly between the two parts.

The text could be used as an additional primary text in vocal/choral, instrumental, and general music education methods courses at the undergraduate and graduate level, introduction to music education courses, and in music courses focusing on multicultural music education. It could also serve as a primary text for a course at the graduate level specifically focusing on culturally responsive approaches to music teaching.

Culturally Responsive Teaching in Music Education: From Understanding to Application also could be used as a supplementary text in a general teacher education course such as Sociology of Teaching and Learning or Anthropology of Teaching and Learning to demonstrate how this approach might be used in music learning contexts. Additionally, it could be a supplementary text for a humanities course, as it focuses on the close relationship between music, culture, and learning.

ACKNOWLEDGMENTS

We are indebted to many people without whose assistance this book would not have been possible. First, we would like to thank our editor, Genevieve Aoki, for helping us to navigate the process of writing a second edition.

We also would like to express appreciation to the following music educators, students, and administrators whose lives and work continue to inspire us: Ellice Amendolare, Marissa Armitage, Mark Dillon, Dwayne Dunn, Lewis Fowler, Kyle Garcia, Vince Genualdi, Lillie Harris, Jason Alexander Holmes, Dawn Humphrey, Kaitlynn Cassio Igari, Jeff Kleiber, Jill Pittman, Emma Rainoff, Pedro Ramos, Marta Richardson, Michael Raiber, and Ron Wakefield.

INTRODUCTION

Why a Book about Culturally Responsive Teaching?

A fundamental premise of teaching is that students are unique in the ways they learn. It is one of the reasons that designing instruction that incorporates a variety of strategies and approaches in order to meet the needs of diverse learning styles is a fairly common practice among teachers. Moreover, our increasingly pluralistic and interconnected world underscores the influence of factors related to race, ethnicity, and culture on student learning.

Numerous educational researchers (Banks, 2019; Gay, 2018; Ladson-Billings, 2017; Nieto & Bode, 2017; Noel, 2017; Paris & Alim, 2017) have acknowledged that today's teachers must be sensitive to and knowledgeable about the influence of race, ethnicity, and culture on learning. This is no less true for music education, particularly given the intimate connection between music and culture. However, we have observed:

> The path to greater understanding is challenging; remedies are not readily apparent and the topic is sensitive in nature. If … we truly believe in music for every child, we must find ways to support teaching and learning for culturally diverse learners.
>
> *(McKoy et al., 2010, p. 52)*

Indeed, we have come a long way over the past two decades in recognizing the importance of cultural diversity in music education. Leading music education researchers and scholars often cite the changing demographics in American schools as the catalyst for new approaches to music teaching and we have seen a tremendous growth in the literature dealing specifically with cultural diversity and music

DOI: 10.4324/9781003208136-1

learning. However, as Schippers (2005) pointed out, whether referring to cultural diversity of content or ethnic diversity of learners, several concepts and ideas have been featured prominently in the discussions but have not been examined critically. Additionally, Schippers noted that terms such as *ethnicity* and *multiculturalism* are frequently used but ill-defined. Because we believe that studying music from a multicultural perspective (both in terms of context and content) is imperative for music education in the 21st century, this text will examine music teaching and learning through the lens of culture.

Conceptual Framework

The framework of this book is based on a conceptual model (see Figure 0.1) that we developed previously with our colleague Dr. Abigail Butler (Butler et al., 2007) and which represents a review and synthesis of research and scholarship on the impact of race, ethnicity, and culture on the teaching and learning process in music. The model consists of five categories: teacher, learner, content, instruction, and context. The categories represent dimensions or constructs (and their respective associated components) that may serve as barriers to or supports for music learning among diverse student populations, depending upon how they are influenced or affected by race, ethnicity, and culture. Though the model as illustrated may suggest that the boundaries between each dimension are discrete, they actually are often blurred: components from one dimension may influence or interact with those from one or more of the other dimensions.

Models such as this can serve several purposes. Following Edwards (1992) and Tuckman and Harper (2012), we indicated three purposes for our model: (1) to codify and organize existing research knowledge; (2) to assist in formulating hypotheses and theories that can guide research; and (3) to investigate relationships between components of specific phenomena in order to predict specific outcomes. The third purpose of a conceptual model is the one that is the most pertinent for this book because, as Tuckman and Harper (2012) have observed, such a model is "a complex proposal of all the variables and their interconnections that make a particular outcome, such as learning … happen" (p. 110).

This conceptual model has been the catalyst for much of our research and scholarship. Together and separately, we have worked to test the model's viability regarding a variety of theories. One theory that we spent a great deal of time with was **culturally responsive teaching**. This theory made sense with our conceptual model, and it provided a way for us to talk about the interactions we had identified as vitally important to music learning, not just in conceptual terms, but in ways that matter in the classroom. By overlaying our conceptual model with the theory of culturally responsive teaching, we were able to identify how the theories and concepts associated with culturally responsive teaching could be applied in a music education context.

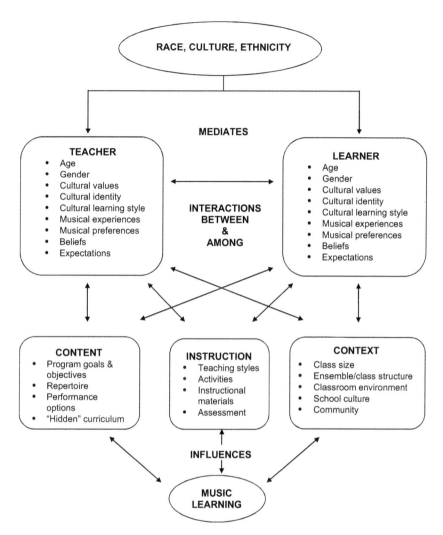

FIGURE 0.1 Conceptual model illustrating dimensions of the music learning process mediated by race, ethnicity, and culture

Assumptions Informing Our Perspective for this Book

In writing a book about culturally responsive teaching in the music classroom, we recognize the danger of oversimplifying the issues associated with it. We understand that an individual's way of learning in music is more than the sum total of a learning style which may be associated with culturally specific ways of knowing. Although our book is designed to provide illustrations and explanations of how culturally responsive teaching can function within music instructional settings, it is not our intention to trivialize culturally responsive teaching or to suggest that it can be achieved by merely following prescriptive procedural steps. The successful application of culturally responsive teaching in a music education context occurs as a result of several factors, including the understanding of the history and principles of the pedagogy, musical content knowledge, effective instructional skills, and appropriate dispositions.

As we formulated our ideas for this text, we made conscious and intentional decisions about what content we would and would not include. For example, because culturally responsive pedagogy is a facet of equitable access and **social justice** in education, these topics may be presented but in limited scope. Our book is not designed to be a philosophical or theoretical treatise on social justice and/or multiculturalism in music education. There are other texts available that are intended to present this information in greater detail.

We also want to clarify that, though culturally responsive teaching shares the same acronym (CRT) as **critical race theory**, the two ideas are distinctly different. Our decision to mark this difference was precipitated by the recent focus on critical race theory in the media due to disinformation that has circulated conflating approaches like culturally responsive teaching with the tenets of critical race theory. Consequently, we have included a glossary in this new edition to help readers distinguish these and additional terms that have recently become more prominent in public discourse over the past few years.

Finally, we acknowledge that race, ethnicity, gender, and culture are just a few of the facets of human diversity. We have chosen to explore these areas in this book because we have focused on them as dimensions of cultural distinction in our own research, and because of their importance in the classroom. We hope this text will cause readers to think more deeply about human diversity and consider ways to make our music classrooms more inclusive and our instruction more meaningful.

References

Banks, J. (2019). *An introduction to multicultural education* (6th ed.). Pearson.

Butler, A., Lind, V. R., & McKoy, C. L. (2007). Equity and access in music education: Conceptualizing culture as barriers to and supports for music learning. *Music Education Research, 9*(2), 241–253.

Edwards, R. H. (1992). Model building. In R. Colwell (Ed.), *Handbook of research on music teaching and learning* (pp. 38–47). Schirmer.

Gay, G. (2018). *Culturally responsive teaching: Theory, research, and practice* (3rd ed.). Teachers College Press.

Ladson-Billings, G. (2017). The (r)evolution will not be standardized: Teacher education, hip hop pedagogy, and culturally relevant pedagogy 2.0. In D. Paris and H. S. Alim (Eds.), *Culturally sustaining pedagogies: Teaching and learning for justice in a changing world* (pp. 141–156). Teachers College Press.

McKoy, C. L., Lind, V. R., & Butler, A. (2010). Conceptually framing teaching and learning within the context of culture: Implications for music teacher education. In M. Schmidt (Ed.), *Collaborative action for change: Selected proceedings from the 2007 Symposium on Music Teacher Education* (pp. 51–70). Rowman & Littlefield.

Nieto, S., & Bode, P. (2017). *Affirming diversity: The sociopolitical context of multicultural education* (7th ed.). Pearson.

Noel, J. (2017). *Developing multicultural educators* (3rd ed.). Waveland Press.

Paris, D., & Alim, H. S. (2017). What is culturally sustaining pedagogy and why does it matter? In D. Paris & H. S. Alim (Eds.), *Culturally sustaining pedagogies: Teaching and learning for justice in a changing world* (pp. 1–24). Teachers College Press.

Schippers, H. (2005). Taking distance and getting up close: The Seven Continuum Transmission Model. In P. S. Campbell, J. Drummond, P. Dunbar-Hall, K. Howard, H. Schippers, & T. Wiggins (Eds.), *Cultural diversity in music education: Directions and challenges for the 21st century* (pp. 29–34). Australian Academic Press.

Tuckman, B. W., & Harper, B. E. (2012). *Conducting educational research* (6th ed.). Rowman & Littlefield.

PART I
Understanding

1

CULTURE, EDUCATION, AND CULTURALLY RESPONSIVE TEACHING

The origins of culture are to be found in music, in dance, and in performance.

John Blacking

Understanding the nature of culture, and the relationship between culture and education provides a necessary foundation for understanding the significance of culturally responsive pedagogy for the teaching and learning process in music. In this chapter, we will (1) discuss the definitions for and the dimensions of culture, (2) investigate education as cultural transmission, (3) review the theoretical development of culturally responsive teaching and culturally sustaining pedagogy, and (4) identify the characteristics of culturally responsive teaching and describe how they function within the specific context of music instruction.

What Is Culture?

Definitions of culture vary depending on the discipline. In the area of anthropology, which involves the study of human beings, one of the earliest definitions of culture was provided by Edward Burnett Tylor. In 1871, he defined culture as "that complex whole which includes knowledge, belief, art, morals, law, custom, and any other capabilities and habits acquired by man as a member of society" (p. 1). Other definitions include:

1. The customary beliefs, social forms, and material traits of a racial, religious, or social group (*Merriam-Webster*, 2022).
2. A set of beliefs, practices, and symbols that are learned and shared. Together, they form an all-encompassing, integrated whole that binds people together and shapes their worldview and lifeways (Brown et al., 2020, p.41).

DOI: 10.4324/9781003208136-3

3. The ideations, symbols, behaviors, values, and beliefs that are shared by a human group. Also, symbols, institutions or other components of human societies that are created by human groups to meet their survival needs (Banks, 2019, p. 165).
4. Belief systems and value orientations that influence customs, norms, practices, and social institutions, including psychological processes (language, care-taking practices, media, educational systems) and organizations (media, educational systems) (American Psychological Association, 2017, p.165).

While the definitions in the list range from general to more detailed, all of them share a common focus on the behaviors or customs, beliefs, and values of groups of human beings. The definitions provided by Banks (2019) and the American Psychological Association (2017) imply that organizations developed for educational, social, religious, or other purposes also comprise culture. Thus, our definition of culture encompasses the actions, attitudes, and formal organizational structures associated with groups of people.

These varying definitions suggest that culture is a complex concept that functions on several levels. Hidalgo (1993) described culture as having three levels: concrete, behavioral, and symbolic. The concrete level represents the most visible and tangible aspects of culture and includes surface dimensions such as food and dress, which often provide the focus for multicultural festivals or celebrations. The behavioral level explains how we define our social roles, the language(s) we speak, and how we approach non-verbal communication. The behavioral level reflects our values and includes such elements as language, gender roles, family structure and political affiliations. The symbolic level is comprised of our values and beliefs. It can be abstract; however, it is the key to how we define ourselves. Components of the symbolic level include value systems, customs, spirituality, religion, and worldview (Hidalgo, 1993).

Two metaphors are frequently used to illustrate the nature of culture: (1) the "iceberg" metaphor and (2) the "tree" metaphor. The iceberg metaphor presents culture as having two aspects: one that is clearly visible or above the surface and a larger aspect that is hidden or beneath the surface (Hall, 1976). Noel (2017, p. 11) describes the tree metaphor similarly:

> Some of these components [of culture] can be visualized as the branches of a tree, as the outward and observable customs of a culture. It is the roots, however, that provide the deeper, shared values and beliefs of which the branches grow. Current definitions of culture focus at the level of the roots of the tree, emphasizing the idea that a culture's values and beliefs will shape the customs and traditions of that culture.

A relationship can be drawn between the "tree" or "iceberg" metaphor for culture and Hidalgo's three levels of culture. The visible portion of the iceberg and the branches of the tree correspond to the concrete level and some aspects of the behavioral level of culture noted by Hidalgo; the hidden portion of the iceberg and the roots of the tree correspond to the aspects of Hidalgo's behavioral and symbolic levels of culture. The iceberg and tree metaphors reiterate the notion that our conception of culture is often regarding visible, surface aspects, and that the deeper, more abstract, less visible components can only be uncovered through interaction with individuals within a culture.

Scholars such as Bennett (2013) argue that the use of static objects to illustrate the nature of culture gives an inaccurate characterization of culture as an entity, rather than "the process whereby groups of people coordinate meaning and action, yielding both institutional artifacts and patterns of behavior" (para. 2). We know that culture is complex; the metaphors above and Hidalgo's levels of culture may be viewed as an oversimplification of cultural concepts. Yet, we have used them here as a starting point for understanding some dimensions of culture, particularly in terms of how we tend to conceptualize other cultures in comparison to our own. For example, our perspective of other cultures often focuses on the artifacts that are the results of cultural processes; when we consider those aspects of our own culture that we would wish others to understand, they often include those deeper, less visible, but perhaps more significant aspects of culture such as our values and beliefs.

Another essential characteristic of culture is that it is influenced by a variety of factors and thus, it is constantly evolving. Noel (2017, p. 15) observed, "A group of people does not have *a* [single] culture, an unchanging and unalterable view of the world. Increasing geographic mobility, access to worldwide media, and new pieces of knowledge contribute to a dynamic conception of culture." Given that our social and cultural experiences form our worldviews, variations in those experiences result in changes in the cultural lens through which we view those experiences.

Of course, when we focus on the nature of culture as it relates to the shared ways in which groups of people may think about and engage with the world, we also run the risk of reducing groups to sets of stereotypical characteristics. It is important to keep in mind that although members of an ethnic or cultural group may share some core cultural characteristics, this does not imply that those characteristics are identically demonstrated by all members of the group (Gay, 2018). Imposing assumptions about the "average characteristics" of a group upon all the individuals in that group results in stereotyping. Striking a balance between awareness of shared core cultural features and values within ethnic and cultural groups, and awareness of the numerous ways in which individuals within an ethnic group may express those characteristics can be challenging. Nevertheless, it is critical to understanding how culture mediates all aspects of human conduct, including the education process.

Culture and Education

Education is a multifaceted enterprise. From a sociological viewpoint, it involves interactions and relationships formed between and among teachers and learners within an organized system. From a psychological perspective, it requires an understanding of the ways in which human beings learn and the types of instructional processes which foster that learning. From an anthropological standpoint, education involves the formal and informal transmission of cultural knowledge. Informal learning takes place daily in family and public settings where individuals learn through imitation and following social models. Formal learning occurs in locations and during events that are culturally endorsed and regulated, such as schools and ceremonies (Conklin, 2002–2004; Erickson, 2010). Thus, every learning situation is mediated by cultural influences and no learning situation is culturally neutral (Wlodkowski & Ginsberg, 1995).

Historically, Western education has been an institution that has influenced cultural change (Rogoff, 2003). In circumstances where the imposition of Western education was forced (i.e., colonization, missionary efforts, or western encroachment in the U.S.), the intent often was to change the cultural practices of the indigenous cultures through the transmission of the practices of the settler culture. In this way, the educational enterprise involved both *enculturation* and *acculturation*. Kim and Abreu (2001) define enculturation as the process of (re)socializing and maintaining the norms of the indigenous culture. Acculturation refers to changes that occur due to contact with culturally dissimilar people, groups, and social influences (Gibson, 2001). In other words, enculturation may be thought of as first-culture learning, while acculturation involves second-culture learning. Although acculturation can be a two-way process, it is frequently understood in terms of the adjustments and adaptations that populations in the minority make in response to their contact with populations in the majority (Sam & Berry, 2010).

Because the school represents one of the formal ways of educating for cultural transmission, it has a specific role to play in the relationship between culture and education. Thomas (2000) differentiated between education and *schooling*, characterizing the former as the realization of an individual's intrinsic goals for personal self-development, and the latter as the realization of extrinsic societal goals.

> Schooling is the process that goes on in the school and can be thought of as a distinctive form of enculturation which is formalised through the curriculum … The rationale for schooling throughout the world is surprisingly universal, *[sic]* schools attempt to engender self-realisation, provide society with citizens that are skilled, knowledgeable, and able to participate in an effective and efficient division of labour, and to act as an agent of intergenerational cultural transmission.
>
> *(Thomas, 2000, p. 25)*

School curricula tend to reinforce and support the ways of knowing, values, norms, and customs of the larger or macro-culture. For example, in the U.S., schools tend to promote themes such as individualism and competition that are valued in the larger society. To the extent that a school curriculum reflects the cultural themes of its learners, it serves to enculturate them by continuing the process of "within culture" knowledge transfer that the learners have experienced from birth. If, however, a curriculum does not reflect or support the cultural knowledge base that learners have acquired, then the educational process is more like acculturation, where learners must adjust the culturally based skills and competencies they have learned and align them with the expectations of the larger culture (Boykin, 2000). This process of acculturation can present difficulties for learners, particularly if measures of academic success do not accommodate their own cultural ways of knowing. As Pai et al. (2006, p. 6) have noted, "There is no escaping the fact that education is a socio-cultural process. Hence, a critical examination of the role of culture in human life is indispensable to the understanding and control of the educative process." In so far as cultural transmission is one purpose of education, understanding culture as a critical variable that influences learners' ways of knowing and perceiving is important. It is an understanding essential to culturally responsive teaching.

The Development of Culturally Responsive Teaching

The roots of culturally responsive teaching may be traced to educational changes precipitated by the 1954 landmark Supreme Court decision in the case of *Brown v. Board of Education*, which outlawed segregation in all U.S. public schools. Prior to this ruling, a policy of racial segregation (commonly known as the doctrine of "Separate but Equal") was predominant in the United States. This doctrine—sanctioned in 1896 by another Supreme Court Case, *Plessy v. Ferguson*—held that as long as separate facilities for Black and White people were equal, segregation did not violate the Fourteenth Amendment, which addresses citizenship rights and equal protection under the law (Kluger, 1975). By 1954, when the Supreme Court was considering the case of *Brown v. Board of Education*, a growing division in the country was evident. Of the 48 U.S. states at the time, 17 states, primarily southern, required racial segregation, while 16 states prohibited it. The remaining 15 states did not have legislation requiring or limiting segregation, but many of these states allowed policies to be implemented in schools and businesses reflecting the "Separate but Equal" doctrine sanctioned by *Plessy v. Ferguson* (Kluger, 1975; Maruca, 2004).

The decision in *Brown v. Board of Education* was significant and required a radical shift in the policies in place across the country. The question placed before the court was not whether segregated schools were equal, but whether the part of the doctrine requiring *separation* was constitutional. In Chief Justice Earl Warren's summary opinion, the longstanding policy supporting segregation was struck down and a new era in the politics of race in America began. In his ruling, the

Chief Justice described why racial separation did not result in equality for many school-aged children.

> Segregation of white and colored children in public schools has a detrimental effect upon the colored children. The impact is greater when it has the sanction of the law, for the policy of separating the races is usually interpreted as denoting the inferiority of the Negro group. A sense of inferiority affects the motivation of a child to learn.
> *(Leadership Conference on Civil and Human Rights, 2015, para. 11)*

The years that followed the *Brown* decision saw a slow but persistent desegregation of public schools. As formerly segregated public-school classrooms began to reflect greater racial, ethnic, and socioeconomic variety, teachers noticed differences in academic achievement among many students (Banks, 2004). The reasons for these discrepancies in achievement were attributed to both racial and socioeconomic factors. Social scientists and educational psychologists began to investigate race and education to explain the disparity in achievement.

One of the first theories to be developed in the early 1960s was the concept of *cultural deficit, deprivation* or *disadvantage*. The cultural deficit model (also known as the cultural deprivation paradigm) held that students' home culture was the key to understanding what was impeding the successful academic achievement of students of color. Thus, proponents of this concept believed that the role of the school was to help students overcome the deficits that were a result of their community experiences and family backgrounds (Bereiter & Engelmann, 1966; Bloom et al., 1965; Crow et al., 1966). The overarching belief was that students who came from poor financial circumstances had no culture to speak of that would assist them in attaining academic success. This perspective was highly influenced by a theory of cultural poverty developed by Oscar Lewis and based on studies he conducted between 1959 and 1968 on people of low income in urban areas in Mexico, New York, Puerto Rico, and Cuba. The culture of poverty Lewis proposed consisted of 70 traits compressed into four clusters: (1) basic attitudes, values, and character structure of people experiencing poverty; (2) the nature of family systems of people experiencing poverty; (3) the nature of poverty-stricken communities; and (4) the social and civic relationship with the larger society of people experiencing poverty (Foley, 1997). In terms of the impact of these "traits" of poverty on academic achievement in school, Bloom et al. (1965, p. 4) observed:

> We refer to this group as culturally disadvantaged or deprived because we believe the root of their problem may in large part be traced to their experiences in homes which do not transmit the cultural patterns necessary for the types of learning characteristic of the schools and the larger society.

Because this perspective characterized the prevailing thinking of the time, cultural deprivation became the dominant paradigm guiding the development of academic programs and pedagogies for low-income populations during the 1960s (Banks, 2004).

By the 1970s and into the 1980s, new voices were beginning to be heard; voices that challenged the previously accepted theories of cultural deprivation and disadvantage. Most prominent among these was Paolo Freire, whose seminal work *Pedagogy of the Oppressed* (1970), called into question previous theories of cultural deprivation. Among other ideas, Freire proposed that education should result in the liberation of the oppressed and should not simply be an extension of the culture of the dominant group.

> One cannot expect positive results from an educational or political action program which fails to respect the particular view of the world held by the people. Such a program constitutes cultural invasion, good intentions notwithstanding.
>
> *(Freire, 1970, pp. 83–84)*

In addition, Freire challenged what he called the "banking model" of traditional education, where students are viewed as empty "accounts" into which knowledge is "deposited." Rather, Freire encouraged the application of a "critical pedagogy" in which teachers and learners analyze, question, and look for deeper meanings and implications in what is taught and how it is taught. Freire viewed education as a political act that cannot be separated from pedagogy.

Other scholars promoted theories of cultural difference contending that, regardless of socioeconomic status, race, or ethnicity, all students had rich cultures and heritages, and that the academic achievement gap was a result of significant cultural conflicts in school experienced by many students from populations in the racial minority (Baratz & Baratz, 1970; Erickson, 1987; Ramirez & Castaneda, 1974; Ryan, 1971; Shade, 1982). Anthropologists, social linguists, and educators who embraced this and similar cultural difference theories surmised that developing stronger links between students' home culture and school might result in improved academic achievement and instructional interactions.

A variety of labels began to appear in the literature as theorists began to explore cultural conflict and schooling. Researchers variously described the pedagogies formulated from their ideas as "culturally appropriate" (Au & Jordan, 1981), "culturally compatible" (Jordan, 1985; Vogt et al., 1987), and "culturally congruent" (Mohatt & Erickson, 1981). Ladson-Billings (1995, p. 467) observed that the common thread among the terms *culturally appropriate, culturally congruent,* and *culturally compatible* was an intent to "accommodate student culture to mainstream culture"; that is, to train students from marginalized groups to "fit in" within the status quo of the dominant society. Although students of color or of low socioeconomic status were not necessarily seen as "victims" of their environments, as suggested by the cultural deprivation paradigm, there was still an expectation that adherence to the dominant cultural patterns was key to academic achievement. There was, however, a line of research being developed that looked at bridging the cultural gap between home and school by valuing and validating students' lived cultural experiences (Cazden & Leggett, 1981; Erickson & Mohatt, 1982, Ladson-Billings, 1995). Referred to as *asset pedagogies* and including such terms as culturally responsive or **culturally relevant pedagogy**, these instructional approaches required a more dynamic instructional interaction as teachers worked to incorporate the cultural experiences of learners into the classroom.

Ladson-Billings was one of the first educational researchers to develop a theoretical framework for what she termed "culturally relevant pedagogy" (1995). While her theory built upon the work of the anthropologists and sociolinguists previously mentioned, there were some differences. Ladson-Billings was concerned specifically with developing a theory that did not have at its core the assumption that the academic achievement of groups perceived to be on the margins of the dominant culture was dependent upon their assimilation to the dominant culture. Rather, she sought to develop a theoretical model of effective pedagogical practice that "not only addresses student achievement but also helps students to accept and affirm their cultural identity while developing critical perspectives that challenge inequities that schools (and other institutions) perpetuate" (1995, p. 469).

Although the influence of cultural difference theory in education increased throughout the 1980s and 1990s, the cultural deprivation paradigm has re-emerged recently in public K–12 education, along with a re-emphasis on social class that once again attempts to establish middle-class attitudes, beliefs, and values as the norm (Banks, 2004; Chitty, 2002). This shift is exemplified in the work of Ruby Payne (2013), author of *A Framework for Understanding Poverty*. In her book, Payne claimed that students of low socioeconomic status have difficulty being academically successful because they belong to a "culture of poverty" characterized by value systems that do not support student achievement in school.

Payne's work has come under criticism by education researchers (Bomer et al., 2008; Gorski, 2008; Ng & Rury, 2006; Redeaux, 2011; Van Der Valk, 2016), who suggest that theories such as these purport to explain academic achievement in terms that do not consider the effects of systemic oppression of certain racially and ethnically minoritized groups. Consequently, they are insufficient to account for all the factors that may negatively influence academic achievement among students from these groups. Thus, in the 21st century, the cultural difference paradigm continues to evolve, primarily due to the work of such scholars as Geneva Gay (2018), Tyrone C. Howard (2020), Bettina Love (2020), Sonia Nieto and Patty Bode (2017), Zaretta Hammond (2015), the continuing work of Gloria Ladson-Billings (2017, 2021), and the recent work of Django Paris (2012) and Paris and Samy Alim (2014, 2017).

The Development of Culturally Responsive Teaching in Music Education

Although movement towards a more culturally responsive pedagogy in music education has been a bit slower than in general education, its roots can likewise be traced to the civil rights movement (Campbell, 2002). Since its inception, school music in the United States focused predominantly on European traditions. Certainly, some exceptions existed, notably the inclusion of spirituals in some schools serving African American students (Southern, 1971/1997), and by the 1950s, jazz bands and some popular youth music began to appear in school music programs. However, most school music programs in the U.S. continued to focus on Western European classical traditions.

As a result of desegregation and an increase in the number of immigrants coming to the U.S. from Latin America and Asia, school populations became more diverse and by the mid-1960s music educators began to see a need to broaden the curriculum. Two landmark events, the Yale Seminar held in 1963 and the Tanglewood Symposium held in 1967, helped frame a shift in music education towards a more inclusive curriculum. Thirty-one musicians, scholars, and classroom teachers participated in the Yale Seminar. Citing the lack of communication between musicologists and music educators, the participants criticized school music as "appalling in quality, representing little of the heritage of significant music" (Mark, 1986, p. 42). School music educators were chastised for neglecting non-Western, early Western, jazz, popular, and folk musics.

The Tanglewood Symposium, sponsored by the Music Educators National Conference (MENC), the Berkshire Music Center, the Theodore Presser Foundation, and the School of Fine and Applied Arts of Boston University, was designed to redefine music education for contemporary American society. Participants in the Tanglewood Symposium met to explore ways to better provide music education during a time of rapid social, economic, and cultural changes. Several committees were formed as part of the symposium, each charged with investigating a topic relevant to music education. The committee focusing on *Music of Our Time* acknowledged that Americans had diverse tastes and that different types of musics had value. Again, music educators were called upon to broaden the curriculum by including diverse musics. A second committee, focusing on *Critical Issues*, suggested teacher education programs should consider the special skills and attitudes required of music teachers working in metropolitan centers. The committee members suggested teacher education programs should look for new ways to recruit teachers to city schools and that these teachers should be trained in real community situations (Mark, 1986).

Throughout the 1970s, music educators saw a growth in resources available for teaching world music (Volk, 1998). Textbooks began to include world music examples and numerous articles began to appear in music education journals specifically dealing with the topic of multicultural music. State curriculum guides and

MENC policies reflected a shift in the profession towards a more inclusive philosophy regarding music content, as illustrated by the 1980 *California Framework for Music*, which stated that one of the purposes of music education was to promote awareness and understanding of the music literature of various national cultures (California State Dept. of Education, 1980). There was, however, a concern that music teachers were not prepared to teach world musics to their students.

Patricia Shehan Campbell outlined the changes that were occurring in music education during the 1980s and 1990s in her article "Music Education in a Time of Cultural Transformation" (2002). Concerts and clinics—sponsored by various professional organizations including MENC, the American Orff-Schulwerk Association, and the American Choral Directors Association—were held across the country specifically to advocate for and teach world music. The International Society for Music Education, established in 1953, also promoted a broader curriculum by not only showcasing world music traditions but also highlighting diverse pedagogical practices.

By the late 20th and early 21st centuries, multicultural music had become an established part of the curriculum in many schools. Textbooks specifically designed to facilitate the inclusion of world music into the music classroom began to appear (Anderson, 1991; Anderson & Campbell, 1989; Campbell et al., 1994; George, 1988) and several publishing companies began to include world music in their catalogues. During this same time, music education researchers began to investigate issues surrounding the inclusion of music from a variety of cultures in education. Studies were conducted investigating teacher attitudes toward non-Western music (Lechner & Barry 1997; Robinson, 1996; Teicher, 1997), student preferences for Western and non-Western musics (Darrow et al., 1987; Fung, 1994; McCrary, 1993; Shehan, 1985), and music teacher preparation (Norman, 1999; Quesada & Volk, 1997).

Broadening the music curriculum did not happen quickly or easily, and the shift was not without its problems. Researchers and music education philosophers began to question whether the profession really understood what was meant by **multicultural music education** and whether the path music educators were on could possibly lead to the desired destination. Many leaders in music education began to express concern that the approach to multicultural music education was one-dimensional, even though the issues surrounding diversity and music learning were quite complex. Miralis (2006) discussed the confusion that existed among researchers and scholars resulting from the lack of clearly articulated goals and fuzzy definitions of terms such as "world music" and "multicultural music education."

> Therefore, one frequently observes an absence of a solid philosophical basis for **multicultural education** and world music pedagogy by practitioners, which in turn leads to superficial experiences that focus more on knowledge

about cultural artifacts and melodies than on the development of appropriate attitudes toward people from various cultures.

(Miralis, 2006, pp. 59–60)

Throughout the late 1980s and early 1990s, scholars began to articulate a stronger philosophy for multicultural music education, a philosophy that foreshadowed culturally responsive pedagogy. David Elliott (1989) wrote about cultural democracy in his article, "Music as Culture: Towards a Multicultural Concept of Arts Education." Countering E. D. Hirsch's concept of cultural literacy and the idea that there was a single identifiable body of music that should be taught in schools, Elliott described the need to understand music's connection to culture. Rather than espousing the goal of learning about the so called "great classics," Elliott connected multicultural music education to experiences that would lead to equal opportunities for diverse students. He observed,

> the major goal of multicultural education is simply this: to ensure that all children, male and female students, exceptional students, as well as students from diverse cultural, social-class, racial, and ethnic groups … [experience] an equal opportunity to learn in school.
>
> *(Elliott, 1989, p. 152)*

The evolution of culturally responsive teaching within the field of music education has been slow, but steady. The profession has moved from a singular focus on music from the Western European classical tradition to recognition of the significance of many music-making traditions around the globe and a mandate to broaden music curriculum content. However, expanding the curriculum to include a variety of musical genres, styles, and systems only addressed one aspect of multiculturalism as related to music and music education. The next phase of multiculturalism in music education would, of necessity, focus on developing understandings about how teachers and learners negotiate influential cultural factors during the education process. The next phase of multiculturalism in music education would need to consider the viability of culturally responsive pedagogy.

Characteristics of Culturally Responsive Pedagogy

As discussed earlier, the cultural difference paradigm has been identified pedagogically by various terms. For this book, we have chosen the term *culturally responsive teaching*. According to Gay (2018, p. 36), culturally responsive teaching involves "using the cultural knowledge, prior experiences, frames of reference, and performance styles of ethnically diverse students to make learning encounters more relevant to and effective for them." Culturally responsive teaching implies the ability to affirm diverse cultural characteristics, perspectives, and experiences and to use these multiple perceptions of reality and ways of knowing to form bridges to new learning and ideas.

According to Gay, six salient features characterize culturally responsive teaching. It is (1) validating, (2) comprehensive, (3) multidimensional, (4) empowering, (5) transformative, and (6) emancipatory.

To validate something means to demonstrate or support the truth or value of it. Culturally responsive teaching is validating to learners and to the learning process in a variety of ways. First, as we indicated earlier in this chapter, it addresses the discontinuities between the culture of home and school that exist for many learners by building "bridges of meaningfulness" between these two environments as well as between "academic abstractions and lived sociocultural realities" (Gay, 2018, p. 37). Culturally responsive teaching acknowledges the value of the cultural heritages of differing groups both in terms of curriculum content and in terms of how these respective cultural legacies influence students' attitudes, dispositions, and ways of learning. Because culturally responsive teaching incorporates information from a wide variety of cultural resources and materials for instructional use in all subjects and skill areas in school, learners recognize that their culturally specific ways of knowing are appreciated, valued, and worthy of attention and exploration in the formal curriculum.

Culturally responsive teaching is comprehensive in that it focuses on teaching the whole child. Expectations for learners' development of knowledge and skills and their continued connection with their cultural identities (both as individuals and regarding shared responsibility for cultural communities) are not taught as separate domains. Rather, they are presented as an integrated whole that pervades the way in which a classroom functions. In addition, the comprehensive nature of culturally responsive teaching recognizes and addresses the cultural nature of human cognition (we discuss this further in Chapter 2). As Hollins (1996, p. 13) has observed, culturally responsive teaching incorporates "culturally mediated cognition, culturally appropriate social situations for learning, and culturally valued knowledge in curriculum content." Thus, culturally responsive teaching focuses on learning as a comprehensive or all-encompassing process, not limited merely to the acquisition of new and decontextualized information.

The multidimensionality of culturally responsive teaching is demonstrated through the many facets of the learning enterprise that it encompasses and influences. These areas include curriculum content, the learning context, the classroom climate, student–teacher relationships, instructional techniques, classroom management, and performance assessments (Gay, 2018). In addition, culturally responsive teaching requires an approach to teaching and learning that goes beyond the surface of understanding and explores the complex nature of learning. It values an interdisciplinary perspective that benefits from "a wide range of cultural knowledge, experiences, contributions, and perspectives" (Gay, 2018, p. 39).

Education that empowers is education that gives learners the capacity not only to be academically competent, but to develop a level of confidence and courage that enables them to become agents of change when change is required. According to Shor (1992, pp. 15–16), empowering education

> approaches individual growth as an active, cooperative, and social process because the self and society create each other … The goals of this pedagogy are to relate personal growth to public life, to develop strong skills, academic knowledge habits of inquiry, and critical curiosity about society, power inequality, and change.

Learning is empowering when it brings learners front and center in the learning process, challenges them to engage with ideas in new ways and take ownership of their learning, fosters their self-efficacy, and continually values their culturally situated knowledge as an important means of achieving academic success, rather than as a barrier to it.

The transformative nature of culturally responsive teaching may be understood both in terms of the curriculum and in terms of the learner. Culturally responsive teaching transforms the curriculum in the way in which it challenges traditional educational practices with respect to learners of color. Often, the curriculum content and classroom instruction of traditional educational practice reflects a cultural hegemony that negatively impacts many learners of color. The longer the students remain in school the more their academic achievement levels decrease, resulting in the development of a tendency toward learned helplessness. Culturally responsive teaching sidesteps this tendency. For the learner, culturally responsive teaching transforms the way they see themselves in terms of their personal efficacy and in relation to their cultural communities and the larger society. As Banks (2008, p. 131) has observed, being transformative means helping students "to develop the knowledge, skills, and values needed to become social critics who can make reflective decisions and implement their decisions in effective personal, social, political and economic action."

Finally, culturally responsive teaching is characterized as being emancipatory because it "lifts the veil of presumed absolute authority from conceptions of scholarly truth typically taught in schools [and suggests that] no single version of 'truth' is total and permanent" (Gay, 2018, p. 43). This feature of culturally responsive teaching is one with which many people may have issues because most of us tend to believe that the canon of knowledge that served as the foundation of our own educational experience within a specific discipline is the exclusive source of all authoritative knowledge in that discipline. The idea that there can be multiple and equally viable perspectives regarding a body of knowledge is a comparatively new one. An additional emancipatory benefit of this inclusive approach to the knowledge base is that it enables learners to find their own voices as they explore issues from multiple perspectives and begin to feel the freedom to be "ethnically expressive" instead of trying to cover up their cultural inclinations so as not to make others uncomfortable or in order to blend into the mainstream (Gay, 2018).

Culturally Sustaining Pedagogy

The components characterizing culturally responsive teaching clearly demonstrate how the approach is designed to build on students' cultural assets and remove the pedagogical barriers that can often interfere with students' learning. Sometimes, however, there can be a disconnect when theoretical concepts and pedagogical models are implemented in teaching practice. Paris (2012) suggested that in practice, **asset-based pedagogies** such as culturally responsive teaching and culturally relevant pedagogy are frequently implemented in superficial ways. He attributes this perfunctory implementation to a tendency to misinterpret what it means to teach in ways that are relevant and responsive to the varying cultures of students. This misinterpretation results in teachers using facets of culturally relevant/responsive pedagogy merely as a "hook" to temporarily pique students' interest while continuing to teach the chosen dominant canon.

For Paris, **culturally sustaining pedagogy** emphasizes the importance of teachers maintaining the thread of cultural relevance and responsiveness throughout the learning process to sustain students' cultures and to diversify what is "worth knowing" within a specific academic discipline. It requires educators to understand how young people "enact race, ethnicity, language, literacy and cultural practices in traditional and evolving ways" (Paris & Alim, 2014, p. 90).

An additional important aspect of culturally sustaining pedagogy is that it recognizes culture as fluid and dynamic. This understanding views cultural communities as consisting of both "elder epistemologies" or cultural practices that have sustained indigenous and communities of color for centuries (Holmes & González, 2017), and the new ways in which youth are reshaping those ways of knowing and being to meet their current cultural and political contexts. Paris and Alim have noted that among other asset pedagogies, culturally responsive teaching has

> too often been enacted by teachers and researchers in static ways that look only to the important ways that racial/ethnic difference was enacted by previous generations. As youth continue to develop new, complex, and intersecting forms of racial/ethnic identification in a world where cultural and linguistic recombinations flow with purpose, we need pedagogies that speak to our shifting cultural realities.
>
> *(Paris & Alim, 2017, p. 9)*

Paris' development of the term "culturally sustaining pedagogy" is significant for all the reasons discussed above. While we will continue to use the terms "culturally responsive teaching" and "culturally relevant pedagogy" throughout our book, we fully embrace Paris' insistence that responding to our students' cultural knowledge in our teaching actually means to sustain that knowledge, value it, and be nimble enough to accommodate those "shifting cultural realities."

Summary

Understanding the significance of culturally responsive pedagogy for teaching and learning in music requires an understanding of the nature of culture, the process of education as cultural transmission, and the historical events that have shaped our approach to educating students from diverse cultural backgrounds in the U.S. We have shown that culture is complex; it is multifaceted and dynamic. We have also shown that shared core cultural values that may be demonstrated by specific cultural groups do not negate the variety of ways in which individuals in a specific cultural group may express those cultural ways of life.

From an anthropological view, education is a formal means of transmitting culture. Whether that transmission serves the purposes of enculturation or acculturation depends on the circumstances and the learners involved. However, in cases where the school curriculum content does not value or reaffirm the cultural ways of knowing demonstrated by specific groups of learners, access to knowledge is limited and the means of cultural transmission becomes a barrier to learning and to learners.

Culturally responsive teaching has developed as a result of educators looking for ways to provide equitable educational experiences for all children. It requires teachers to develop strategies designed to connect schooling to the lives and learning styles of culturally diverse student populations. Culturally responsive teaching celebrates diversity and sees it as an instructional resource rather than a problem; it teaches the whole child and integrates all facets of the learning process and the instructional environment; it enables students to develop a sense of self-efficacy both within and beyond school; it challenges the educational status quo for the benefit of all learners; and it acknowledges the importance of including multiple perspectives in the quest to examine and explore the "truths" of a discipline.

Over the past several decades, we have come to a much better understanding of the complexities of teaching and learning, and researchers have well documented the impact of race, ethnicity, and culture on learning. Music teachers have the capacity to move beyond materials and repertoire to delve more deeply into the intricacies of culturally situated musical expression. In the remaining chapters of this part of the book, we will take a closer look at the facets of culturally responsive pedagogy as they relate to the teacher, the learner, and the classroom environment. This foundational understanding will help to set the stage for our discussion of applications in Part II.

Questions for Discussion

1. When you encounter other cultures, which of Hidalgo's three levels of culture do you use in understanding that culture? Is the level you use different from the level you would want others to use in understanding you culturally? If so, what might account for the difference?

2. Discuss some ways in which education might serve to acculturate specific groups of learners.
3. What kinds of situations might qualify as barriers to equitable access in music education?
4. Do you believe that the music you associate with your own ethnic and cultural heritage was reflected in the music curriculum you studied at any educational level? If so, how? If not, describe if or when you became aware of the omission.
5. What societal events other than the ones listed in the review of the development of culturally responsive teaching in music might account for the changes that occurred in music education over the time period mentioned?
6. Why do you think the cultural deficit paradigm is experiencing a resurgence in some areas of education in the U.S. today?
7. Based on your experiences in school, in what ways might there be gaps or discontinuities between the culture of school and the culture of some learners? What are some examples?
8. Have you had experiences that called into question ideas, beliefs, or bodies of knowledge that you previously held to be irrefutable? How did you react?
9. How can culturally responsive teaching validate diverse students' lived experiences?
10. How does culturally sustaining pedagogy address the disconnect between the original theoretical concept of culturally responsive pedagogy, and how it is frequently implemented in schools?

References

American Psychological Association (2017). *Multicultural guidelines: An ecological approach to context, identity, and intersectionality.* www.apa.org/about/policy/multicultural-guideli nes.pdf

Anderson, W. (1991). *Teaching music with a multicultural approach.* MENC.

Anderson, W., & Campbell, P. (1989). *Multicultural perspectives in music education.* MENC.

Au, K., & Jordan, C. (1981). Teaching reading to Hawaiian children: Finding a culturally appropriate solution. In H. T. Trueba, G. P. Guthrie, & K. H. Au (Eds.), *Culture and the bilingual classroom: Studies in classroom ethnography* (pp. 139–152). Newbury House.

Banks, J. A. (2004). Multicultural education: Historical development, dimensions, and practice. In J. A. Banks (Ed.), *Handbook of research on multicultural education* (2nd ed., pp. 3–29). Jossey-Bass.

Banks, J. A. (2008). *Teaching strategies for ethnic studies* (8th ed.). Pearson.

Banks, J. A. (2019). *An introduction to multicultural education* (6th ed.). Pearson Education.

Baratz, S. S., & Baratz, J. C. (1970). Early childhood intervention: The social science base of institutional racism. *Harvard Educational Review, 40*(1), 29–50.

Bennett, M. J. (2013, May 6). Culture is not like an iceberg [web log post]. www.idrinstit ute.org/page.asp?menu1=14&post=1&page=1

Bereiter, C., & Engelmann, S. (1966). *Teaching disadvantaged children in the preschool.* Prentice Hall.

Bloom, B. S., Davis, A., & Hess, R. (1965). *Compensatory education for cultural deprivation.* Holt, Rinehart, & Winston.

Bomer, R., Dworin, J. E., May, L., & Semingson, P. (2008). Miseducating teachers about the poor: A critical analysis of Ruby Payne's claims about poverty. *Teachers College Record, 110*(12), 2497–2531.

Boykin, A. W. (2000). The talent development model of schooling: Placing students at promise for academic success. *Journal of Education for Students Placed at Risk, 5*(1&2), 3–25.

Brown, N., McIlwraith, T., & Tubelle de González, L. (2020). *Perspectives: An open introduction to cultural anthropology* (2nd ed.). American Anthropological Association.

California State Dept. of Education (Ed.). (1980). *Visual and performing arts framework.* Author.

Campbell, P. S. (2002). Music education in a time of cultural transformation. *Music Educators Journal, 89*(1), 27–32, 54.

Campbell, P. S., McCullough-Brabson, E., & Tucker, J. (1994). *Roots and branches: A legacy of multicultural music for children.* World Music Press.

Cazden, C., & Leggett, E. (1981). Culturally responsive education: Recommendations for achieving Lau remedies II. In H. Trueba, G. Guthrie, & K. Au (Eds.), *Culture and the bilingual classroom: Studies in classroom ethnography* (pp. 69–86). Newbury.

Chitty, C. (2002). Education and social class. *The Political Quarterly, 73*(2), 208–210.

Conklin, K. R. (2002–2004). Education transmits a culture. www.angelfire.com/hi2/hawaiiansovereignty/edtransmitsculture.html

Crow, L. D., Murray, W. I., & Smythe, H. H. (1966). *Educating the culturally disadvantaged child: Principles and programs.* David McKay.

Darrow, A., Haack, P., & Kuribayashi, F. (1987). Descriptors and preferences for Eastern and Western musics by Japanese and American nonmusic majors. *Journal of Research in Music Education, 35*, 237–248.

Elliott, D. (1989). Music as culture: Toward a multicultural concept of arts education. *Journal of Aesthetic Education, 24*(1), 147–166.

Erickson, F. D. (1987). Transformation and school success: The politics and culture of educational achievement. *Anthropology and Education Quarterly, 18*, 335–356.

Erickson, F. (2010). Culture in society and in educational practices. In J. A. Banks & C. A. M. Banks (Eds.), *Multicultural education: Issues and perspectives* (7th ed., pp. 33–56). Wiley.

Erickson, F., & Mohatt, G. (1982). Cultural organization and participation structures in two classrooms of Indian students. In G. Spindler (Ed.), *Doing the ethnography of schooling* (pp. 131–174). Holt, Rinehart & Winston.

Foley, D. E. (1997). Deficit thinking models based on culture: The anthropological protest. In R. R. Valencia (Ed.), *The evolution of deficit thinking: Educational thought and practice* (pp. 113–131). The Stanford Series on Education and Public Policy. Routledge-Falmer.

Freire, P. (1970). *Pedagogy of the oppressed.* Continuum International Publishing Group

Fung, V. (1994). Undergraduate nonmusic majors' world music preference and multicultural attitudes. *Journal of Research in Music Education, 42*, 45–57.

Gay, G. (2018). *Culturally responsive teaching: Theory, research, and practice* (3rd ed.). Teachers College Press.

George, L. A. (1988). *Teaching the music of six different cultures.* World Music Press.

Gibson, M. A. (2001). Immigrant adaptation and patterns of acculturation. *Human Development, 44*, 19–23. https://doi.org/10.1159/00005703

Gorski, P. C. (2008). Peddling poverty for profit: Elements of oppression in Ruby Payne's framework. *Equity and Excellence in Education, 41*, 130–148.

Hall, E. T. (1976). *Beyond culture.* Anchor Books.

Hammond, Z. (2015). *Culturally responsive teaching and the brain.* Generic.

Hidalgo, N. (1993). *Multicultural teacher introspection.* Routledge.

Hollins, E. R. (1996). *Culture in school learning: Revealing the deep meaning.* Lawrence Erlbaum Press.

Holmes, A. & González, N. (2017). Finding sustenance: An indigenous relational pedagogy. In D. Paris & H. S. Alim (Eds.), *Culturally sustaining pedagogies: Teaching and learning for educational justice in a changing world* (pp. 207–224). Teachers College Press.

Howard, T. C. (2020). *Why race and culture matter in schools: Closing the achievement gap in America's classrooms* (2nd ed.). Teachers College Press.

Jordan, C. (1985). Translating culture: From ethnographic information to educational program. *Anthropology and Education Quarterly, 16*, 105–123.

Kim, B. S. K., & Abreu, J. M. (2001). Acculturation measurement: Theory, current instruments, and future directions. In J. G. Ponterotto, J. M. Casas, L. A. Suzuki, & C. M. Alexander (Eds.), *Handbook of multicultural counseling* (2nd ed., pp. 394–424). Sage Publications.

Kluger, R. (1975). *Simple justice: The history of Brown v. Board of Education and Black America's struggle for equality.* Alfred A. Knopf Publishers.

Ladson-Billings, G. (1995). Toward a theory of culturally relevant pedagogy. *American Education Research Journal, 32*, 465–491.

Ladson-Billings, G. J. (2017). "Makes me wanna holler": Refuting the "culture of poverty" discourse in urban schooling. *The ANNALS of the American Academy of Political and Social Science, 673*(1), 80–90.

Ladson-Billings, G. J. (2021). I'm here for the hard reset: Post pandemic pedagogy to preserve our culture. *Equity and Excellence in Education, 54*(1), 68–78.

Leadership Conference on Civil and Human Rights. (2015). *Brown v. Board of Education (Kansas).* www.civilrights.org/education/brown/brown.html

Lechner, J., & Barry, N. (1997). Multicultural education through art, literature, and music: A study of preservice teachers' perceptions of appropriate materials and methods. *Journal of Research and Development in Education, 30*(2), 87–102.

Love, B. (2020). *We want to do more than survive: Abolitionist teaching and the pursuit of educational freedom.* Beacon Press.

Mark, M. (1986). *Contemporary music education.* Schirmer.

Maruca, M. (2004). *Brown v. Board of Education historical handbook.* Western National Parks Association.

McCrary, J. (1993). Effects of listeners' and performers' race on music preferences. *Journal of Research in Music Education, 41*(3), 200–211.

Merriam-Webster. (2022). Culture. In *Merriam-Webster.com.* www.merriam-webster.com/dictionary/culture

Miralis, Y. (2006). Clarifying the terms "multicultural," "multiethnic," and "world music education" through a review of literature. *Update: Applications of Research in Music Education, 24*(2), 54–66.

Mohatt, G., & Erickson, F. (1981). Cultural differences in teaching styles in an Odawa school: A sociolinguistic approach. In H. Trueba, G. Guthrie, & K. Au (Eds.), *Culture and the bilingual classroom: Studies in classroom ethnography* (pp. 105–119). Newbury House Publishers.

Ng, J. C., & Rury, J. L. (2006). Poverty and education: A critical analysis of the Ruby Payne phenomenon. *Teachers College Record, 110*(12), 2497–2531. www.tcrecord.org/Content. asp?ContentID=12596

Nieto, S., & Bode, P. (2017). *Affirming diversity: The sociopolitical context of multicultural education* (6th ed.). Pearson Education.

Noel, J. (2017). *Developing multicultural educators.* Waveland Press.

Norman, K. (1999). Music faculty perceptions of multicultural music education. *Bulletin of the Council for Research in Music Education, 139,* 38–49.

Pai, Y., Adler, S. A., & Shadiow, L. K. (2006). *Cultural foundations of education* (4th ed.). Merrill/Prentice Hall.

Paris, D. (2012). Culturally sustaining pedagogy: A needed change in stance, terminology, and practice. *Educational Researcher, 41*(3), 93–97. https://doi.org/0.3102/0013189X1 2441244

Paris, D., & Alim, H. S. (2014). What are we seeking to sustain through culturally sustaining pedagogy? A loving critique forward. *Harvard Educational Review, 84*(1), 85–100.

Paris, D., & Alim, H. S. (2017). *Culturally sustaining pedagogies: Teaching and learning for justice in a changing world.* Teachers College Press.

Payne, R. K. (2013). *A framework for understanding poverty* (4th ed.). aha! Process.

Quesada, M., & Volk, T. (1997). World musics and music education: A review of research, 1973–1993. *Bulletin of the Council for Research in Music Education, 131,* 44–66.

Ramirez, M., & Castaneda, A. (1974). *Cultural democracy, bi-cognitive development and education.* Academic Press.

Redeaux, M. (2011). A framework for maintaining White privilege: A critique of Ruby Payne. *Counterpoints, 402,* 177–198. www.jstor.org/stable/42981082

Robinson, K. M. (1996). *Multicultural general music education: An investigation and analysis in Michigan's public elementary schools, K–6.* Unpublished doctoral dissertation, University of Michigan.

Rogoff, B. (2003). *The cultural nature of human development.* Oxford. University Press.

Ryan, W. (1971). *Blaming the victim.* Vintage Publishing.

Sam, D. L., & Berry, J. W. (2010). Acculturation: When individuals and groups of different cultural backgrounds meet. *Perspectives on Psychological Science, 5,* 472–481. http://doi. org/10.1177/1745691610373075

Shade, B. (1982). Afro-American cognitive style: A variable in school success? *Review of Educational Research, 52,* 219–244.

Shehan, P. (1985). Transfer of preference from taught to untaught pieces of non-western genres. *Journal of Research in Music Education, 33*(3), 149–158.

Shor, I. (1992). *Empowering education: Critical teaching for social change.* University of Chicago Press.

Southern, E. (1971/1997). *The music of Black Americans: A history.* W. W. Norton & Company.

Teicher, J. (1997). Effect of multicultural music experience on preservice elementary teachers' attitudes. *Journal of Research in Music Education, 45*(3), 415–427.

Thomas, E. (2000). *Culture and schooling: Building bridges between research, praxis and professionalism.* Wiley Publishing Company.

Tylor, E. B. (1871). *Primitive culture: Researches into the development of mythology, philosophy, religion, art, and custom, vol. 1.* Bradbury Press.

Van Der Valk, A. (2016). Questioning Payne. *Learning for Justice Magazine, 52.* https://www.learningforjustice.org/magazine/spring-2016/questioning-payne

Vogt, L., Jordan, C., & Tharp, R. (1987). Explaining school failure, producing school success: Two cases. *Anthropology and Education Quarterly, 18*(4), 276–286.

Volk, T. M. (1998). *Music, education, and multiculturalism: Foundations and principles.* Oxford University Press.

Wlodkowski, R. J., & Ginsberg, M. B. (1995). *Diversity and motivation: Culturally responsive teaching.* Jossey-Bass.

2

UNDERSTANDING HOW CULTURE INFORMS THE DEVELOPMENT OF TEACHERS

We teach who we are.

Parker Palmer

The quality of teaching is central to the learning process. Consequently, if increased student learning is to be achieved, then a focus on the teacher as a key agent in the teaching and learning enterprise is essential. This chapter focuses on: (1) how pre-service and in-service music teachers' cultural backgrounds influence their development as teachers; (2) defining cultural competence and its relationship to culturally responsive teaching; and (3) how cultural competence and racial/ethnic awareness can be acquired and fostered in pre-service music teachers to increase their instructional effectiveness in culturally diverse educational settings.

Who "We" Are

Since we wrote the first edition of this book, little has changed in the demographic makeup of the American teaching force. A report from the National Center for Education Statistics estimated there were 3.5 million full- and part-time teachers working in American schools during the 2017–18 school year. Approximately three quarters of the teachers were female, and the average age was 42 years old. These figures give us interesting statistical data, and they do give us an image of our profession, but just as we cannot assume all of our students are alike, we cannot generalize about who is teaching in the classroom. We can, however, recognize the trends and work to better understand ourselves in relationship to these trends.

One important consideration when looking at culturally responsive teaching is the ethnic and cultural backgrounds of our teachers. Historically, American schools have had a homogeneous teaching and student population and, although

DOI: 10.4324/9781003208136-4

the student population in PreK–12 schools has become more diverse, the teaching force has remained static over the past several decades. In 2017–18, the percentage distribution of U.S. public school students by race or ethnicity in grades PreK–12 was 47% White, 15% Black, 27% Hispanic, 5% Asian, <1% Pacific Islander, 1% American Indian/Alaska Native, and 4% two or more races (National Center for Education Statistics, 2021). In comparison, the percentage distribution of U.S. public school PreK–12 *teachers* by race or ethnicity for 2017–18 was 79% White, 7% Black, 0.5% American Indian/Alaska Native, 2% Asian, <1% Pacific Islander, 9% Hispanic, and 1% multiracial (National Center for Education Statistics, 2021).

Looking at the data on teacher and student enrollment, we find that teachers of a given race do tend to teach in schools with a student body that matches their own, however, the majority of the teaching force in most schools continues to be White. There is still a considerable dissimilarity between the cultural backgrounds of many public-school students, and the cultural backgrounds of their teachers, and this disparity may be greater in the music classroom. In a 2015 article, Kenneth Elpus reported that between 2007 and 2012, music teacher licensure candidates identified as 86.02% White, 7.07% Black, 1.94% Hispanic, 1.79% Asian, 0.3% Native American/Alaska Native, 0.32% Pacific Islander, 0.82% multiracial, and 1.74% other.

Both pre-service and in-service teachers often harbor subconscious beliefs, attitudes, and misperceptions about students from cultural backgrounds that differ from their own that are based on prejudice and preconception. Research conducted in the late 1990s and early 2000s suggested that these attitudes and beliefs are responsible for some teachers' lack of commitment to teach in schools with culturally diverse populations and preference for teaching in monocultural educational settings (Bradfield-Kreider, 2001; Dieker et al., 2002; Nierman et al., 2002; Wiggins & Follo, 1999). More recent research indicates that not much has changed. Starck et al. (2020) found that both teachers and non-teachers held pro-White implicit and explicit racial biases, and the teacher bias level was found to be related to student outcomes. The work of other researchers (Kunesh & Noltemeyer, 2019; Shannon-Baker, 2020; Sleeter, 2017) similarly indicates that the racial bias of pre-service teachers negatively affects how they interact with students of color and negatively impacts student outcomes.

Kelly (2003) looked specifically at music teaching and had similar findings. Many pre-service and in-service music teachers wanted to teach in educational settings that mirror their own experiences. If they attended suburban high schools that were not particularly racially or ethnically diverse, but which had exceptional music programs, that is the type of school in which they wanted to teach. Though many pre-service music teachers say they are comfortable with the idea of teaching in ethnically and racially diverse educational environments, they are ambivalent about the actual possibility of teaching in such environments (McKoy, 2006). Most in-service music teachers say they believe in the importance of multicultural music education and teaching music in a culturally responsive way, yet their curricula and teaching practices do not always reflect an understanding of what that might look like (Abril, 2013; Legette, 2003). The difference between the cultural backgrounds of students, and this teachers who instruct them is well documented, and this gap is growing as the student population becomes more diverse.

As a result of this demographic shift, music teacher education programs have been called upon to prepare teacher candidates to work in culturally diverse settings (McKoy, 2009). Standards set forth for the teaching profession by both the Council for the Accreditation of Educator Preparation (CAEP) and the National Association of Schools of Music (NASM) require programmatic components be developed to address issues of diversity (CAEP, 2020; NASM, 2021). The NASM specifically states that prospective teachers should develop "The ability to maintain positive relationships with individuals of various social and ethnic groups and be empathetic with students and colleagues of differing backgrounds" (NASM, 2021, p. 120). This attribute, often referred to as cultural or cross-cultural competence, is widely acknowledged as a crucially important component of successful teaching (Seeberg & Minick, 2012; Williams, et al., 2016).

Understanding and Fostering Cultural Competence

"**Cultural competence**" implies the capacity to function effectively within the context of the cultural beliefs, behaviors, and needs presented by consumers and their communities (National Center for Cultural Competence, 2020). In the context of education, cultural competence is reflected in teachers who can function, communicate, and coexist effectively in settings with individuals who possess cultural knowledge and skills that differ from their own. Additionally, culturally competent teachers affirm the varied and unique cultural experiences, values, and knowledge their students bring to the classroom, and they use these resources as tools to teach more effectively, thereby increasing student learning and achievement.

Derald Wing Sue has been a leader in the field of psychology and cultural competence over the past 30 years. Along with several colleagues, Sue developed a conceptual framework to help organize the many complex and interrelated dimensions of cultural competence (Sue, 1990, 1991, 2001; Sue et al., 2019). This work parallels the work being done in education and serves as a useful tool for identifying the components of cultural competence that relate to what teachers need to know and be able to do in the classroom. The three attributes associated with cultural competence for psychologists were identified as awareness, knowledge, and skills. When placed in the context of education, culturally competent teachers work to: (1) develop an awareness of self, of assumptions, values, and biases; (2) learn about culturally diverse populations and seek to understand the sociopolitical and structural barriers that impede learning for culturally diverse populations; and (3) develop appropriate instructional strategies and techniques (Sue et al., 1992).

Assumptions, Values, and Biases

The first key component to developing cultural competence requires teachers to understand their own cultural conditioning and recognize that this conditioning affects their personal beliefs, values, and attitudes (Gallavan, 2011; Gay, 2015; Howard, 2020). Most of us like to believe we are fair and objective when working with students. In reality, all of us are shaped by our experiences and cultural heritage, and we make explicit or implicit assumptions based on those lived experiences.

In Chapter 1, we discussed how a deficit-based approach to addressing cultural difference in education was generated from a misperception that students who were not academically successful were culturally deprived; that is, they had insufficient experience with the values and knowledge of the dominant culture. Despite the problems with this view of cultural difference, many teachers today are still largely biased in favor of mainstream ways of learning and instruction, which, in turn, bias their perceptions regarding students in the classroom (Gay, 2018). In other words, students who follow mainstream classroom practices in terms of how they behave and learn during class time are perceived as highly motivated and are seen as more highly achieving than are students exhibiting more ethno-cultural ways of behaving and learning. Additionally, these same instructional biases inform and negatively influence how teachers perceive and evaluate the learning abilities of students who may display alternative or ethno-cultural classroom values (Boykin et al., 2006; Gay, 2018; Tyler et al., 2006; Villegas & Lucas, 2002). Thus, a teacher's bias in favor of mainstream instructional practice and ways of knowing can reinforce biased attitudes and beliefs the teacher may hold about members of racial, ethnic, and cultural groups.

To overcome the effect of bias in the classroom, teachers must recognize their own assumptions. This can only happen when teachers engage in critical self-reflection and self-assessment. Before we can deal with cultural bias in the classroom, we must recognize it in ourselves and acknowledge that our actions reflect both our conscious and our subconscious beliefs. Engaging in critical self-reflection, however, is not easy. Howard (2020) described the difficult task of developing a mindset for critical self-reflection as one that requires teachers to ask challenging questions related to their own views regarding race and culture. It requires teachers to consider whether they hold conscious or subconscious deficit-based beliefs about certain groups of students. As noted earlier, most teachers in the music classroom are White. A painful, yet necessary component of critical self-reflection for this majority population is to recognize the privileged status of members of the dominant group. To change the practices that have led to the disenfranchisement of certain populations, we must begin to understand the nuances of our teaching and determine how our decisions are rooted in our own experiences and how these decisions affect our students.

One of the greatest obstacles to critical self-reflection is the belief that there is a single "right" way of teaching and learning (Lynch, 2011). Many of us attended traditional schools where desks were arranged in straight rows and students were asked to remain silent for most of the day. These traditions were reinforced during our pre-service education by faculty who had, likewise, been enculturated into the established norms of our education system. Yet, there are other ways of providing education; we must learn to question the details of our system and be open to the realization that there are many ways of teaching. In *The Moral Life of Schools*, the authors stated that every detail in schooling, "from the interior of the principal's office to the way the school's cafeteria operates, from the school-wide policy that governs the giving of grades to the rules that deal with the way students move through the halls, can be examined with an eye to moral significance" (Jackson et al., 1998, p. xviii). We contend that these details are not only moral in nature but are a result and reflection of our own cultural heritage. The extent to which these details impede or support learning among culturally diverse populations can only be determined through critical self-evaluation. The "right" way will not look the same for all students, but must be crafted to fit the learning styles, cultural heritage, and individual needs of our students.

Understanding Culturally Different Learners

According to Sue et al. (2019), the second step to developing cultural competence is to broaden one's worldview. To craft a system based on different norms, we will have to expand our concept of what those norms could and should look like. Developing cultural competence requires that we get to know more about the culture of our students, learn about their worldview, and work to better understand their expectations for schooling. Building on our capacity to create a classroom that reflects different cultural norms requires that we better understand the possibilities for change, and critically examine the rationale for our current practices.

Coming to a better understanding of teaching often requires challenging the dominant paradigm by considering different ways of knowing and learning as "different from" but not deficient to others. Developing a true understanding of diverse cultures is hard work. Teachers must be willing to spend time reading about and observing the traditions and behaviors of diverse cultural groups and they must continually filter the interpretations of what they see and read through an understanding of their own personal bias. Knowing about the traditions, customs, music, ways of communicating, and patterns of behavior of different cultural groups requires intense study. However, building upon our knowledge of others is a critical step in designing and implementing educational practices that more effectively meet the needs of all students (Gay, 2018; Howard, 2020; Lynch, 2011).

Developing Appropriate Instructional Strategies and Techniques

Ultimately, the goal of culturally responsive pedagogy is to improve the academic experiences of all students by providing equitable experiences in the classroom. We can re-envision our classrooms in ways that allow us to move away from an exclusively Eurocentric model to a more inclusive process, one that allows all students opportunities to access learning in ways that are respectful and congruent with different ways of knowing. For music education, this involves broadening the curriculum to include diverse music genres and looking at different ways of promoting or even defining musicality.

Music study at the college level traditionally has emphasized the development of knowledge and performance proficiency in terms of the Western European classical repertoire. Over the past two decades, there has been a more inclusive philosophy in some institutions of higher education and study now includes American music and non-Western music traditions. However, college music program entrance requirements still focus on classical training and the ensemble model promotes traditional practices. With the shift towards an increasingly diverse PreK–12 curriculum, it is imperative that pre-service music teachers have experiences learning about and performing music outside the Western European classical tradition. Certainly, musicians trained in the Western canon but whose racial and ethnic backgrounds have afforded them extended study and performance of music that is not a part of the traditional canon have demonstrated the capacity for bi-musicality or the capacity to function efficiently in more than one musical system. For example, trumpeter Wynton Marsalis effectively performs music within Western European classical genres and American jazz genres. However, bi-musicality as a curricular objective is not the norm in many music schools across the country. The current approach to diversity in the content of the music curriculum may be giving music teacher candidates a false perception of their readiness to teach the music of other cultures effectively and may lead them to believe that culturally diverse music content is irrelevant to their professional and instructional goals and objectives.

Given that music-making and music education in some world macro- and micro-cultures do not necessarily occur in the kinds of institutional settings that are most frequently associated with formal music education in Western society, music teachers should be encouraged to consider that music learning can, and often does occur in many different instructional contexts. Music teachers can learn to become facilitators of their own as well as their students' learning by identifying opportunities to gain musical knowledge beyond the four walls of the music classroom. Music educators may be the experts in the music they have been trained to understand and perform, but both their students and the culture bearers/cultural informants in the communities in which they will teach may be the experts in other forms of musical expression, and music teachers should be encouraged to seek out the resources they need to "fill in the gaps" where their own knowledge may be insufficient.

In the article, "Being the Other: Adapting to Life in a Culturally Diverse Classroom," Benham (2003) discussed his experiences teaching an elementary string class in a school located in an urban area, where he found himself perceived as a cultural "outsider" by his students. Moreover, he discovered that the strategies and approaches to teaching that had been successful in other instructional environments were not effective for his students. He slowly developed an awareness of the need to understand the norms, expectations, and values of the school and community in which he taught, which ultimately helped him to communicate more effectively as a teacher. Benham is not alone in feeling like an outsider; many teachers work in settings that are not congruent with their experiences or expectations. Likewise, many of our students do not "fit in" with the current model of schooling and, as a result, struggle throughout their school-aged years. Unfortunately, there is a tendency for us to blame students for the disconnect, assuming their lack of engagement is their fault.

Why Cultural Competence Matters

When we critically examine the issue of equal access in education, there can be no question that the opportunities and outcomes for students in the racial minority in American schools have differed and continue to differ from those of their White, middle-class counterparts (Banks, 2004; Howard, 2020; Kozol, 1991). The term *achievement gap* has been used for several years when referring to the disparity in academic success (e.g., grades, test scores, and graduation rates) and educational opportunities (e.g., expulsion and suspension rates, placement in special education, and access to advanced courses) for certain groups of students when compared to the dominant culture. As the number of students in the ethnic/racial minority has continued to grow, so has the achievement gap.

Numerous articles and book chapters have focused on the achievement gap among school-aged students, looking for possible causes and hoping to find solutions to the problems (Gay, 2005; Howard, 2020; Lee, 2002). Scholars have cited gaps in reading readiness (Howard, 2020; Lee, 2002), lower teacher expectations (Irvine & York, 1993), cultural differences among majority and minority populations (Gay, 1995), and discrepancies in school funding (Darling-Hammond, 2007; Howard, 2020), as possible factors. Jonathan Kozol (1991, 2005) has spent much of his career writing about educational inequalities and in his text, *The Shame of a Nation* (2005), he described the discrepancies in per-student spending among urban and suburban schools, the deplorable conditions of schools in many urban centers, and the "gross discrepancies" in teacher salaries between those working in the city and those in the more affluent White suburbs. Banks et al. (2005) further documented inequalities in education when looking at class size and the qualifications of the teaching force.

A History of Disenfranchisement

The inequality that exists in funding for education certainly matters, but it is not the only contributing factor to discrimination in education. Historical and socio-political components that framed our educational institutions have and continue to play a role in creating the current gap in educational opportunities. Ladson-Billings (2006) argued that these factors have created an educational debt that has accumulated over time and the debt must be addressed if we truly want to see change. Before we can address this debt, however, we must acknowledge the history that led us here.

The inequalities that have existed in American schooling are well documented for African American, Native Indian, and Latinx students. African Americans were forbidden any type of education during the years of slavery, and after emancipation, schools were developed to maintain a servant class (Ladson-Billings, 2006). Prior to desegregation, African American children were given second-hand textbooks and relied on materials that were discarded by White schools. African American children living in the rural south attended schools during academic years that were typically four months long. African American educators and parents valued education and worked to provide educational opportunities for African American youth under extremely restrictive circumstances (Ladson-Billings, 2006; Walker, 2000).

The history of schooling for Native American students is likewise filled with flagrant inequalities. Early education for Native Americans was provided through mission schools. These schools were created to convert Native Americans and to develop a labor force for the church. Beginning in 1887, the American government began building boarding schools for the express purpose of assimilating Native American youth. The students were forbidden to use their Indian names, were not allowed to speak in their native language, and male students were forced to cut their hair. The forced assimilation is perhaps best illustrated in the words of Captain Richard H. Pratt, founder of the Carlisle Barracks.

> A great general has said that the only good Indian is a dead one, and that high sanction of his destruction has been an enormous factor in promoting Indian massacres. In a sense, I agree with the sentiment, but only in this: that all the Indian there is in the race should be dead. Kill the Indian in him, and save the man.
>
> *(Barrows, 1892, p. 46)*

According to a documentary directed by Christine Lesiak, assimilation did not mean equality; many of the Native American graduates of the boarding schools found they no longer fit in on the reservation, yet they were not welcome in White society (Lesiak, cited in Ladson-Billings, 2006).

Latinx students also share a history of discrimination in both policy and practice and have suffered from "a long tradition of segregation" in public schools (Ferg-Cadima, 2004). During the late 1880s, as Mexican and Mexican American workers began to migrate northward looking for work, communities began to implement restrictive policies limiting access to public facilities. In the southwest, strict segregation policies were in place and by 1930, 85% of Mexican children attended school in either separate classrooms or separate schools. The "Mexican School" facilities were described as substandard with broken windows, cracks in the walls, and rooms without lighting, and the school year was substantially shorter than the neighboring *Anglo* schools. In districts that did not segregate Latinx students, a *de facto* segregation often resulted from the age difference among the students. Latinx children often struggled to meet grade level expectations and as a result, were placed in classes with much younger children. In 1934, 70% of Latinx students in Santa Ana County, California were classified as "retarded" because they were older than the typical student at their grade level. Many students were 16 by the time they reached the eighth grade and school attendance was no longer mandatory. Thus, the failure to promote pushed Latinx students out of the education system (Ferg-Cadima, 2004).

Although policies in the U.S. began to shift in the 1960s, the sociopolitical climate in this country continued to serve as a barrier to equality and equity in education. Families of color often advocated for improvements in schooling, but their voices were marginalized and largely ignored by the politically powerful (Ladson-Billings, 2006). *Brown v. the Board of Education* changed American policy, yet it did not change the practice in many large urban school districts across the country. By 2001, 90% of Chicago public-school students were Black or Hispanic; 94% of the students in Washington, DC were Black or Hispanic, and in Detroit, less than 5% of the public-school students were White (Kozol, 2005). Historically, this pattern has been reflected in many large metropolitan areas across the country and it continues to be the norm for many urban school settings today.

Summary

Teachers who demonstrate proficiency in culturally responsive pedagogy and who have developed cultural competencies are sensitive to the complex issues surrounding inequality in education. Culturally competent teachers get to know their communities and work to better understand their students, and they use their knowledge of others to better design and implement curricula that reflect an understanding of and appreciation for diverse ways of being and knowing.

We believe that teachers can develop a firm foundation based on the following principles.

1. No culture is better than another, nor is one way of knowing "right" or "wrong."

2. Culture is complex; for most of us, a superficial definition of culture is insufficient to characterize our humanity. We do not necessarily belong to a single cultural group (though we may self-identify with one or two).
3. We are all unique; we reflect our cultural heritage, but we are influenced by a myriad of factors.
4. Stereotypes do little to help us understand the students in our classroom and can interfere with our ability to understand each student's unique perspective.
5. By referring to "different" cultures, we acknowledge there are ways of perceiving, knowing, and being that are different from our own. We understand "different" does not mean "better than" or "worse than."
6. Diversity is an asset; something to be valued.
7. Culture is not static. We are all products of our heritage, circumstances, and experiences. Over time, we all change and adapt.
8. Historical and sociopolitical factors have influenced the structure of schooling and continue to impact our work as teachers.

There is no "quick fix" for teachers looking for ways to develop and incorporate culturally responsive teaching strategies. Rather, teachers must work to examine their own practices and develop strategies that are appropriate for all of the students in their classroom. To develop culturally responsive teaching strategies, teachers must critically examine all aspects of teaching and learning, including content, process, and classroom environment, while considering the individual needs of their students.

Sue et al. (2019) outlined several strategies for developing the skills identified above. Adapting his strategies for music education, we recommend teachers seek out professional development opportunities that focus on multicultural music and working with diverse students. State and national music education conferences offer numerous workshops and in-service programs specifically highlighting multicultural music, and several universities offer courses in specific types of world musics. Music teachers can also benefit from participating in in-service opportunities in general education focusing on diversity. We also recommend teachers seek out and read books and articles focused on topics relevant to cultural competence, specifically ones dealing with the unique characteristics of cultures and their musics.

Perhaps the most important step in developing cultural competence is learning to act upon our knowledge of ourselves and others to develop skills that are congruent with diverse learners. It is not enough to reflect upon our own learning and to explore different ways of knowing; we must act upon what we learn. Freire (1970) stated that teaching is a political act; it is never neutral. If we begin to consider every action that we take in our classroom as a moral action and if we understand that these actions have consequences that will be different for various populations, we can better develop strategies that meet the needs of all our students.

The teacher is one of the primary agents in the educational process. As previously noted, the quality of teaching, among other factors, can make the difference between students who are highly motivated and deeply engaged with the subject matter and those who find no relevance or meaning in the subjects they are expected to learn. In the case of culturally responsive pedagogy, the quality of teaching is dependent upon each teacher's willingness to consider the various ways in which their cultural background, beliefs, attitudes, and certain aspects of professional preparation may interfere with or inhibit their ability to teach a culturally diverse student population effectively. The development of cultural competence is one way to help mitigate the negative impact that these factors can have on the teaching and learning process when the ethnic, racial, and cultural backgrounds of teachers and students differ dramatically.

Cultural competence is particularly salient for music educators because music and culture are intimately connected. People use music to establish personal and social identity. Music serves a variety of functions that are at once common across cultures and uniquely specific to each one. Thus, when music teachers seek to develop cultural competencies, they will gain the tools they need to "assist them in valuing the varying culturally-specific knowledge bases and musical ways of knowing that their students bring to the music classroom and using these varying points of reference to facilitate and maximize student learning in music" (McKoy, 2009, p.142). In other words, their teaching will become culturally responsive.

Questions for Discussion

1. How were your ideas about teaching formed?
2. What are the ways in which your beliefs and traditions impact your teaching?
3. How do your beliefs and traditions impact your ability to work with students who are different from you?
4. What are some examples of implicit bias that may impact music teaching and learning?
5. What music do you value? How does your musical preference impact what you view as being worthy of study?
6. How do today's schools reflect the history of racial and ethnic discrimination?
7. What strategies can you employ to develop cultural competence?

References

Abril, C. (2013). Toward a more culturally responsive general music classroom. *General Music Today, 27*(1), 6–11.

Banks, J. A. (2004). Multicultural education: Historical development, dimensions, and practice. In J. A. Banks & C. A. M. Banks (Eds.), *Handbook of research in multicultural education* (2nd ed., pp. 2–29). Jossey-Bass.

Banks, J. A., Cochran-Smith, M., Moll, L., Richert, A., Zeichner, K., LePage, P., Darling-Hammond, L., & Duffy, H. (2005). Teaching diverse learners. In L. Darling-Hammond

& J. Bransford (Eds.), *Preparing teachers for a changing world: What teachers should learn and be able to do* (pp. 232–274). Jossey-Bass.

Barrows, I. C. (Ed.) (1892). *Proceedings of the national conference of charities and corrections at the nineteenth annual session held in Denver, Col., June 23–29, 1892.* Boston Press. http:// quod.lib.umich.edu/n/ncosw/ACH8650.1892.001?rgn=main;view=fulltext

Benham, S. (2003). Being the other: Adapting to life in a culturally diverse classroom. *Journal of Music Teacher Education, 13*(1), 21–32.

Boykin, A. W., Tyler, K. M., Watkins-Lewis, K. M., & Kizzie, K. (2006). Culture in the sanctioned classroom practices of elementary school teachers serving low-income African American students. *Journal of Education of Students Placed At-Risk, 11*(2), 161–173. https://doi.org/10.1207/s15327671espr1102_3

Bradfield-Kreider, P. (2001). Personal transformations from the inside out: Nurturing monocultural teachers' growth toward multicultural competence. *Multicultural Education, 8*(4), 31–34.

Council for the Accreditation of Educator Preparation. (2020). *CAEP accreditation standards.* Author. http://caepnet.org/standards/2022-itp/introduction

Darling-Hammond, L. (2007, May 21). Evaluating "No Child Left Behind": The problems and promises of Bush's education policy. *The Nation.* www.thenation.com/article/eva luating-no-child-left-behind#

Dieker, L., Voltz, D. & Epanchin, B. (2002). Report of the Wingspread Conference: Preparing teachers to work with diverse learners. *Teacher Education and Special Education, 25*(1), 1–10.

Elpus, K. (2015). Music teacher licensure candidates in the United States: A demographic profile and analysis of licensure examination scores. *Journal of Research in Music Education, 63*(3), 314–335.

Ferg-Cadima, J. (2004). *Black, White and Brown: Latino school desegregation efforts in pre- and post-Brown v. Board of Education era.* Mexican American Legal Defense and Education Fund. http://inpathways.net/LatinoDesegregationPaper2004.pdf

Freire, P. (1970). *Pedagogy of the oppressed.* Continuum.

Gallavan, N. (2011). *Navigating cultural competence in grades K–5: A compass for teachers.* Corwin Press.

Gay, G. (1995). Mirror images on community issues. In C. Sleeter & P. McLaren (Eds.), *Multicultural education, critical pedagogy and the politics of difference* (pp. 155–190). State University of New York Press.

Gay, G. (2005). Politics of multicultural teacher education. *Journal of Teacher Education, 56*(3), 221–228.

Gay, G. (2015). The what, why, and how of culturally responsive teaching: International mandates, challenges, and opportunities. *Multicultural Education Review, 7*(3), 123–139.

Gay, G. (2018). *Culturally responsive teaching: Theory, research, and practice* (3rd ed.). Teachers College Press.

Howard, T. C. (2020). *Why race and culture matter in schools: Closing the achievement gap in America's classrooms* (2nd ed.). Teachers College Press.

Irvine, J. J., & York, D. E. (1993). Teacher perspectives: Why do African-American, Hispanic, and Vietnamese students fail? In S.W. Rothstein (Ed.), *Handbook of schooling in urban America* (pp. 161–173). Greenwood Press.

Jackson, W. J., Boostrom, R. E., & Hansen, D. T. (1998). *The moral life of schools.* Jossey-Bass.

Kelly, S. N. (2003). The influence of selected cultural factors on the environmental teaching preference of undergraduate music education majors. *Journal of Music Teacher Education, 12*(2), 40–50.

Kozol, J. (1991). *Savage inequalities*. Crown Books.

Kozol, J. (2005). *The shame of a nation*. Crown Books.

Kunesh, C., & Noltemeyer, A. (2019). Understanding disciplinary disproportionality: Stereotypes shape pre-service teachers' beliefs about lack boys' behavior. *Urban Education, 54*(4), 471–498.

Ladson-Billings, G. (2006). From the achievement gap to the education debt: Understanding achievement in U.S. schools. *Educational Researcher, 35*(7), 3–12.

Lee, J. (2002). Racial and ethnic achievement gap trends: Reversing the progress toward equity. *Educational Researcher, 31*(1), 3–12. http://69.8.231.237/uploadedFiles/Journals_ and_Publications/Journals/Educational_Researcher/3101/3101_Lee.pdf

Legette, R. M. (2003). Multicultural music education attitudes, values, and practices of public-school music teachers. *Journal of Music Teacher Education, 13*(1), 51–59.

Lynch, J. (2011). Educating diverse learners through culturally responsive instruction. In J. Edim (Ed.), *Essays in helping diverse students attain educational success* (chap. 3). The Edwin Mellen Press. www.academia.edu/1231455/Educating_Diverse_Learners_through_ Culturally_Responsive_Instruction

McKoy, C. L. (2006). Pre-service music teachers' cross-cultural awareness, exposures and attitudes: A preliminary study. *Southern Music Education Journal, 2*(1), 78–94. http://libres. uncg.edu/ir/uncg/f/C_McKoy_Pre-service_2006.pdf

McKoy, C. L. (2009). Cross-cultural competence of student teachers in music education. In S. Cooper (Ed.), *The Journal of the Desert Skies Symposium on Research in Music Education 2009 Proceedings* (pp. 128–144). University of Arizona. http://libres.uncg.edu/ir/uncg/ f/C_McKoy_Cross_2009.pdf

National Association of Schools of Music. (2021). *NASM competencies summary: The baccalaureate degree in music education, a professional undergraduate degree*. Author. https://nasm. arts-accredit.org/wp-content/uploads/sites/2/2021/01/O_Baccalaureate-Degree-in-Music-Education.pdf

National Center for Cultural Competence. (2020). *Conceptual frameworks/models, guiding values and principles*. Author. https://nccc.georgetown.edu/foundations/framwork.php

National Center for Education Statistics, U.S. Department of Education. (2021). *Report on the characteristics of public-school teachers* (NCES 202144). Author. https://nces.ed.gov/ programs/coe/indicator/clr

Nierman, G. E., Zeichner, K., & Hobbel, N. (2002). Changing concepts of teacher education. In R. Colwell & C. Richardson (Eds.), *The new handbook of research on music teaching and learning* (pp. 818–839). Oxford.

Seeberg, V., & Minick, T. (2012). Enhancing cross cultural competence in multicultural teacher education: Transformation in global learning. *International Journal of Multicultural Education, 14*(3), 1–22.

Shannon-Baker, P. (2020). Those who can't hear must feel: Confronting racism, privilege, and self with pre-service teachers. *Theory into Practice, 59*(3), 300–309. http://doi.org/ 10.1080/00405841.2020.1740020

Sleeter, C. (2017). Wrestling with problematics of whiteness in teacher education. *International Journal of Qualitative Studies in Education, 29*(8), 1065–1068.

Starck, J. G., Riddle, T., Sinclair, S., & Warikoo, N. (2020). Teachers are people too: Examining the racial bias of teachers compared to other American adults. *Educational Researcher, 49*(4), 273–284. https://doi.org/10.3102/0013189X20912758

Sue, D. W. (1990) Culture specific techniques in counseling: A conceptual framework. *Professional Psychology: Research and Practice, 21*(6), 424–433.

Sue, D.W. (1991) A model for cultural diversity training. *Journal of Counseling and Development, 70*(1), 99–105.

Sue, D. W. (2001). Multidimensional facets of cultural competence. *The Counseling Psychologist, 29*(6), 790–821.

Sue, D. W., Arredondo, P., & McDavis, R. (1992). Multicultural counseling competencies and standards: A call to the profession. *Journal of Multicultural Counseling and Development, 20*(2), 64–88.

Sue, D. W., Sue, D., Neville, H. A., & Smith, L. (2019). *Counseling the culturally diverse* (8th ed.). Wiley.

Tyler, K. M., Boykin, A. W., & Walton, T. R. (2006). Cultural considerations in teachers' perceptions of student classroom behavior and achievement. *Teaching and Teacher Education, 22*(8), 998–1005. https://doi.org/10.1016/j.tate.2006.04.017

Villegas, A. M., & Lucas, T. (2002). Preparing culturally responsive teachers: Rethinking the curriculum. *Journal of Teacher Education, 53*(1), 20–32.

Walker, S. W. (2000). Valued segregated schools for African American children in the south, 1935–1969: A review of common themes and characteristics. *Review of Educational Research, 70*(3), 253–285.

Wiggins, R., & Follo, E. (1999). Development of knowledge, attitudes and commitment to teach diverse student populations, *Journal of Teacher Education, 50*(2), 94–105.

Williams, J., Price, R. F., DeLaney, M., Green, D. H., Minigan-Finley, P., Finey, T., & Yates, L. (2016). Cultured pearls: A phenomenological investigation of the pedagogical practices of culturally responsive White teachers in urban schools. *Proceedings of the American Education Research Association: Public Scholarship to Educate Diverse Democracies, held in Washington, DC.*

3

UNDERSTANDING HOW CULTURE INFORMS LEARNERS' EXPERIENCES IN THE MUSIC CLASSROOM

If our system doesn't have a place where a child fits, there's something wrong with the system, not the child.

William G. Defoore

Like teachers, learners bring a wide variety of personal experiences, beliefs, attitudes, and expectations into the music classroom. Understanding how culture mediates all these factors during learners' musical experiences is critical for educators interested in maximizing student learning through culturally responsive teaching. Chapter 3 focuses on issues illustrating how learning, both in general and in relation to music, is mediated by race, ethnicity, and culture. Because an understanding of child development is critical to any discussion of learning, we begin with an examination of how child development and cognition function within a variety of cultural contexts. Then, using a cultural lens, we examine other factors that inform students' music learning experiences.

Child Development and the Integration of Biology and Culture

Children differ in the ways they learn. The reasons for these differences are multifaceted, and include not only the wide range of physical, cognitive, social, and emotional changes that occur as learners mature but also how these domains are integrated with culture. Thus, sociologists, anthropologists, and a growing number of educators are now questioning the previous mutually exclusive nature/nurture dichotomy as an explanation for human development and are embracing the notion of a connection between biology and culture.

DOI: 10.4324/9781003208136-5

Recent ideas about child development and learning view biology and culture as working simultaneously and in synchronization rather than functioning separately (Gauvain & Munro, 2012; Gutierrez & Rogoff, 2003; Mistry, 2013). Rogoff and Angelillo (2002, pp. 78–79) observed:

> The well-known nature/nurture debate places culture and biology in opposition. Proponents argue that if something is cultural, it is not biological, and if something is biological, it is not cultural. In particular, psychologists have spent a long time trying to figure out what percentage of a person's characteristics is biological and what percentage is cultural or environmental. This artificial separation treats biology and culture as independent entities rather than viewing humans as biologically cultural.

Lev Vygotsky was one of the first to develop a cultural-historical theory of learning that focused on how cultural practices influence cognitive processes. Vygotsky (1978) believed that how people reason, remember, and solve problems is impacted by the ways in which they function in their cultural communities, and therefore, social engagement and communication are important facets of cognitive development. Thus, thinking "depends on features of the context, not just on the mental activity of the brains" (Correa-Chávez & Rogoff, 2005, pp. 7–8).

Those who subscribe to the notion that biology and culture are mutually exclusive tend to view variations across communities as cultural, while similarities are considered biological. In contrast, those who believe that biology and culture are interconnected view human development as building on a foundation of historical legacy and inheritance into which people are born as both "members of their species and members of their community" (Rogoff, 2003, p. 81). Characteristics that we share as human beings, such as using language for communication and developing and using tools, are due to the biological and cultural heritages we share as a species. Likewise, variations across humanity, such as differences in visual and aural acuity, physical strength, family organization, or being familiar with specific languages, are due to differences in both biological and cultural circumstances. As Rogoff (2003, p. 80) has noted, "Similarities and differences across communities do not divide phenomena into biological and cultural." The concept of "nature" and "nurture" as two separate entities influencing human development is an unnecessary bifurcation of a unified process.

Cognition and Culture

Thinking or cognition refers to the mental activities involved in learning. Benjamin Bloom's Taxonomy of the Cognitive Domain (revised by Anderson and Krathwohl in 2001) presents these mental activities in a hierarchy that includes (from lower to higher order thinking) remembering, understanding, applying, analyzing, evaluating, and creating. Traditionally, cognition has been considered a solitary process, which may be influenced by culture, but which primarily functioned independently of it. Now, however, cognitive development is viewed quite differently, based on Vygotsky's assertion that cognitive development is closely related to cultural experience and occurs as people learn to use cultural tools for thinking. In this sense, cognitive development is not the acquisition of knowledge and skills, but rather, it involves

> individuals changing their ways of understanding, perceiving, noticing, thinking, remembering, classifying, problem setting and solving, planning and so on—in shared endeavors with other people building on the cultural practices and traditions of communities. Cognitive development is an aspect of the transformation of people's participation in sociocultural activities.
>
> *(Rogoff, 2003, p. 253)*

Viewing the development of cognition in this way provides new insights into how thinking processes vary across cultural communities. Theories about human development, including cognitive development, have characteristically been based upon research conducted in middle-class communities in Europe and North America. Information from this research is then assumed to be applicable to all people. However, cultural researchers have shown that perceptions about what children are able to do and when they are able to do it vary across cultural communities (Rogoff, 2003; Watson-Gegeo, 1990), bringing into question the generalizability of Western theories of cognitive development. As Rogoff et al. (2017, p. 877) have observed:

> Although mainstream research has begun to include people from a variety of cultural backgrounds, it has seldom adjusted its procedures and interpretation of data to be appropriate to the cultural experience of the participants. Instead, data are often gathered and interpreted from the perspective of the cultural values and practices of the researchers. This is a serious problem— it undermines understanding and negates strengths of individuals and of cultural communities, by judging others' practices by the assumptions and value system of the dominant community.

The results of early research have suggested there are numerous reasons why performance on certain cognitive tasks might not be consistent across different cultures. One reason is the level of familiarity with the task to be performed. For example, children in Zambia performed better on a task involving reproduction of a pattern if they used materials with which they were familiar (i.e., wire instead of paper and pencil). English children did better with paper and pencil. Both groups performed equally well with clay, a medium familiar to both (Serpell, 1979). Other studies revealed strong relationships between the extent of participants' Western education and performance on specific cognitive tasks, suggesting that the types of skills that are typically assessed in cognitive tests are the very skills fostered in Western schooling (Cole, 1990; Rogoff, 1981; Wagner & Spratt, 1987).

The differences in performance on such tasks observed across cultures is more likely to result from the differences in familiarity with common formats and activities of Western schooling used in cognitive tests than on specific cognitive deficits. Take classification tasks, for instance. Studies have shown that people who have had Western schooling categorized items based on their similarity (such as grouping pictures of different kitchen pots together). People who did not have Western schooling tended to classify items based on their function (such as grouping a picture of a kitchen pot with a picture of a stove because the stove is used to cook food in a pot).

Whether a task is situated within a specific cultural context or is decontextualized also impacts performance. For example, in tests of memory, people who had Western schooling tended to be more successful in strategizing ways to memorize disconnected items (Cole et al., 1971; Cole & Scribner, 1977; Scribner, 1974). However, when the ability to memorize was assessed based upon everyday cultural contexts, people without Western schooling could demonstrate extraordinary memory. The griots of West Africa, for example, have maintained oral histories and events spanning hundreds of years.

Cultural differences in performances on tests of intelligence may also be explained by how cultures vary in their interpretation of a problem and by what is considered culturally "appropriate" when working to solve a problem (Goodnow, 1976; Lieberman, 1997). Differences may also be explained by what a culture values (Rosado-May et al., 2020). Some cultural communities value speed in solving problems; others do not. Technical skill is valued by some communities, such as middle-class European American groups, while other groups may value social and emotional skills. Rather than being a singular cognitive process, some cultures perceive intelligence as an integrated combination of characteristics such as wisdom, morality, responsibility, and cleverness, all of which are used for the benefit of the group rather than solely for personal gain.

Knowledge Construction

The mental activities engaged during cognition result in knowledge construction, a dynamic and active process that involves making sense of new information and ideas. As we noted in our discussion of constructivist learning theories in Chapter 1, our understanding of new information and experiences is highly dependent upon the knowledge we already have, which has been filtered through our own frame of reference. To put it another way, we learn by taking new information and experiences and making sense of them based upon the knowledge, beliefs, and skills we already have. In the previous section, we have shown how cognition is culturally situated. Thus, we gain access to learning through our pre-existing knowledge, derived from personal and cultural experiences.

We know that students who bring a different knowledge base to the learning process are often seen as "lacking"; they are viewed through a lens that emphasizes their perceived deficits *when measured by middle-class standards*. Pierre Bourdieu's (1986) theory of cultural capital may be one explanation for why deficit thinking regarding students of specific racial and ethnic backgrounds is so persistent in U.S. education. Bourdieu's theory states that the educational system privileges middle-class students because they possess knowledge and skills that are valued by teachers. Most students are very perceptive about how they are viewed by teachers, and they quickly recognize which teachers value their knowledge and skills and which teachers do not. When what they know and can do is not valued in education, students resist schooling, and engage in what Kohl (1991) calls "not-learning."

> Not-learning tends to take place when someone has to deal with unavoidable challenges to her or his personal and family loyalties, integrity, and identity. In such situations, there are forced choices and no apparent middle ground. To agree to learn from a stranger who does not respect your integrity causes a major loss of self. The only alternative is to not-learn and reject the stranger's world.
>
> *(Kohl 1991, pp. 315–316)*

It is important to consider that students who do not see themselves as being adept at learning what is required by the educational system can become disengaged in a process that continually fails to value their culturally specific knowledge base. Unfortunately, when the resources that students bring to the classroom are overlooked, their access to the knowledge construction process is denied (Villegas & Lucas, 2002; Villegas et al., 2012). However, when students are in educational settings where they can associate new content with their own experiences, and where they can explore and experiment, they are likely to become active participants who can find meaning in their learning (Byrd, 2016; Marlowe & Page, 1999). According to Villegas and Lucas (2002, p. 73), "The content of the curriculum becomes 'knowledge' for students only when they infuse it with meaning."

When we consider the interconnected nature of biology and culture in the context of child development, the wide variations in how cultural communities define cognition, how thinking processes differ across cultures and how knowledge construction is filtered through cultural frames of reference, we can better understand culture as a fundamental dimension of the learning process. As we grow in our knowledge of how culture mediates learning for our students, we gain deeper glimpses into who our students are.

Aural Learning in Music

An important consideration for music educators when looking at knowledge construction is how humans learn music. In music education, we often use phrases such as "sound before symbol" and "rote to note" to indicate that learners should have frequent and extended aural engagement with music in order to understand the syntax of musical communication before they are expected to decode music staff notation. This learning sequence is patterned after the ways in which language acquisition and reading occur. Despite what we state is important in the sequencing of music learning, in reality, the push for learners to read staff notation often begins before they have an opportunity to understand how elements interact in the music they are most familiar with. Our undergraduate music education students often cite music literacy (being able to read, write, and sing notation) as an overarching goal for their teaching and many elementary teachers begin note-reading activities as early as kindergarten and first grade.

This premature focus on reading staff notation may be fueled by several factors, including a tacit subscription to a paradigm that focuses on "notational centricity" or equating "music" with notated music (Lilliestam, 1996, p. 196). Many music teachers believe that the only "right way" to learn music is through notation and "dismiss learning music by ear as a simplistic and inefficient alternative" (Woody, 2012, p. 83), believing that the only *true* musicians are those who can read staff notation.

This rationale derives, in large part, from a focus on traditional performing ensembles (i.e., band, chorus, orchestra) in the music curricula of middle and high school music programs where the notated music of the Western European classical canon has traditionally held sway. It is then reinforced in higher education where entrance exams to music programs focus on music reading skills and graduation requirements reflect similar Western traditions to those found in most of our schools. Woody (2012, p. 82) described how our reliance on notation actually excludes us from developing other facets of musicianship and ultimately results in the devaluation of the ear, "the musician's ultimate asset." Considering that oral transmission of music and playing "by ear" is the typical mode of music-making across cultures and centuries, and that it is the way in which our initial engagement with music occurs, aural learning as a viable option for learners in music takes on a greater significance.

> What we call "oral transmission" is what most human beings throughout history have known simply as "music"—something to play or hear rather than something to write or read. We modern Westerners are the ones who do things differently, and our preference for writing is our handicap.
>
> *(Jeffrey, 1992, p. 124)*

Woody (2012) has noted that of the five musical skills of improvising, performing rehearsed music, playing by ear, playing from memory, and sight-reading, playing by ear was the only one that contributed to the other four skills. This is largely due to the relationship of aural learning to the development of audiation, which Gordon (1999) described as the musical equivalent of thinking in language. Thus, if music learning is analogous to language acquisition and development, then learners would benefit from extensive exposure to aural models and opportunities to imitate those models. Once learners attain performance fluency, they can begin to learn notation. The advantage of this approach is that students bring meaning to the notation based upon their aural experiences, rather than being asked to draw meaning from the notation without the benefit of any musical context from which to construct meaning.

Not only is developing students' aural acuity good educational practice, but it is also a way to honor what many of our students bring to the classroom. Many of our students that engage in music outside of school have learned music through an aural tradition. Regrettably, students whose ways of learning music and whose musical skills stem from an aurally based instructional model often find themselves at odds with formal instruction in music and they feel they have no place in "school music." Mills and McPherson (2006, p. 156) observed that:

1. There are many models of music-making in which notation plays no part.
2. No child needs to be able to decode staff notation accurately *before* learning to make the sorts of music where staff notation is used customarily.
3. Learning to read music before, or separately from, learning to make music can lead to misunderstandings. [...]
4. Undue emphasis on staff notation can lead to atrophy of musicians' creative abilities, and their ability to memorize.
5. Some people who do not read music at all nevertheless become fluent even within the realm of the music where composers and performers customarily use staff notation.

By tapping into oral/aural traditions we can show that we value what students bring to the classroom and we can continue to support their musicianship by connecting with what they already know. Additionally, because music is a part of who we are as humans, connecting to music traditions outside of school can help us better understand our students.

Identity

We have seen the role that culture plays in human cognitive development and in how we construct knowledge. The concept of identity is another factor which influences how our students experience learning in our music classrooms.

Identity, self-concept, and self-esteem are interrelated concepts: they all are facets of the "self," which Baumeister defines as "the totality of you, including your body, your sense of identity, your reputation (how others know you), and so on" (2005, p. 247). They are not, however, interchangeable. Each contributes in a different way to our sense of self. One definition of identity is "the distinctive character belonging to any given individual, or shared by all members of a particular social category or group" (Rummens, 2001, p. 3). Identity is a definition of the self that "is shared by the person, other people, and society at large" (Baumeister, 2005, p. 268). Thus, identity is at once personal and sociocultural. Across the multiple definitions that exist for identity, researchers typically emphasize features that relate to how individuals construct themselves in relation to one or more phenomena. Depending on the roles we choose to adopt at any given time, each of us can have several identities, none of which is singular or discrete; all of which frequently merge and are constantly evolving.

Interestingly, there are intimate connections between the experience of the self and the experience of engagement with music. Frith (1996, p. 109) has drawn an intriguing parallel between the two processes:

> our experience of music—of music making and music listening—is best understood as an experience of [the] self-in-process. Music, like identity, is both performance and story, describes the social in the individual and the individual in the social, the mind in the body and the body in the mind.

Frith's statement points strongly to the significance of music to our identity development. As Cook (1998, p. 5) has observed, "'Music' is a very small word to encompass something that takes as many forms as there are cultural or sub-cultural identities."

MacDonald et al. (2002) noted that music is a way in which we develop both our personal or individual identities and our social identities. The authors proposed two types of musical identity: Identity in Music (IIM), which includes "those aspects of musical identities that are socially defined within cultural roles and musical categories" (p. 2) and Music in Identity (MII), wherein music is used "as a means or resource for developing other aspects of our individual identities" (p. 2). In other words, there are non-musical factors that impact whether and to what extent we identify ourselves as musicians (IIM). Music also plays a role in the development of facets of our identity that are not specifically musically related (MII). Both types of musical identity are mediated by sociocultural factors. Most recently, Elliott and Silverman (2017) have offered an additional facet of musical identity that takes into consideration the idea that the performative and social aspects of music also contribute to the formation of identity. A detailed discussion of each of these facets of musical identify development follows.

Culture and the Development of Musical Identity (IIM)

According to Lamont (2002), musical identity in children emerges around seven years of age and is based on specific activities within music, as well as the influence of parents' attitudes about music and music involvement. Lamont also suggested that students' self-identity as musicians is dependent upon whether they have had formal instruction or not. Children who have studied music privately are more likely to identify themselves as musicians and are more likely to have a positive attitude toward school music. On the other hand, students often do not view themselves as musicians if they have not had formal private study, even though they may play instruments in a music classroom context. Thus, for a child to define himself or herself as a "non-musician" early in life may preclude further development regardless of the child's actual level of potential ability. "The crucial point is that children's self-ratings of musical ability determine the likelihood of their pursuing further activities in music, which in turn provide the opportunities for any progress and development that might take place" (MacDonald et al., 2002, p. 14).

While it may be true that learners who do not or cannot accept "musician" as a possible identity early in life may be engaged in a self-fulfilling prophecy regarding their musical development, the impact of formal music training on the choice to identify as "musician" bears some additional consideration. Although MacDonald et al. appear to be referencing private instruction when they use the term "formal musical training," there is something to be said for other types of learning contexts which may positively impact students' self-concept as musicians, even though that identity may not be reinforced in the school music learning environment. For example, consider the learner who is well-versed in African American gospel music and is an exceptional performer in that musical style. Gospel music is not a primary component of most school vocal/choral music programs and in some circumstances, it is a music style viewed as detrimental to and in conflict with traditional curricular goals and objectives relating to vocal development in music. Nevertheless, the learner who sings gospel music is viewed as an accomplished musician in specific church and community contexts. Such students may very well identify themselves as musicians, but only at particular times and in particular places, and often, the time is not the school day, and the place is not the school classroom.

Our self-concept as "musicians" or of being "musical" is critically influenced by our social and cultural surroundings and by the ways in which we interact with and relate to the people around us (Green, 2002; MacDonald et al., 2011). Prior to attending school, learners' identities, including their developing musical identities, are influenced by parents, family members, and other significant people in their lives. Musical identity continues within the context of school, where teachers and the school environment have a significant bearing on musical identity development, and on motivation as well. According to MacDonald et al. (2011, p. 466),

> children's motivation to succeed in music is inextricably linked with aspects of their musical identity: the ways in which they think about their own abilities have a direct influence upon their motivation to engage in activities which develop those abilities and vice versa.

We may surmise that when definitions of "musician," "musicianship," and who is "musical" are sufficiently broad to encompass a variety of cultural models in the music classroom, learners will benefit.

Music and the Development of Cultural and Individual Identity (MII)

We have noted that developing an understanding of how race, ethnicity, and culture mediate learners' identity development is an important educational consideration (Butler et al., 2007). Racial/ethnic identity represents the extent to which people feel close to their racial or ethnic background and believe that their race/ethnicity is a significant and integral part of their larger identity (Perreira et al., 2010). Although the development of racial and ethnic identity begins in childhood, research indicates that adolescents' identification with their racial and/or ethnic background is associated with higher levels of motivation in school and gives meaning to their academic efforts (Chavous et al., 2003; Fuligni et al., 2005; Oyserman et al., 2001).

Similar to the ways in which identification and affiliation with specific racial or ethnic groups serves to promote healthy self-concepts among individuals, music plays a critical role in the establishment of identity within and across cultural communities. Music has been and continues to be a source of identity for cultural groups and communities and is among several expressive forms that provide opportunities for these groups and communities to be known and understood (McKoy, 2009). According to Folkestad (2002), development of musical identity is a consequence of the variety of contexts (cultural, ethnic, religious, and national) in which people live. Although music can serve to identify us culturally in terms of our affiliation with specific groups, it is important to note that we can and often do choose to move between and among several cultural identities. Likewise, our musical identities, as related to culture, are equally fluid. Thorsen (2002, p. 18) explains it this way:

> A person constantly constructs—according to heritage and aspirations— an individual identity. Added to this we today often find persons who can express a double or multiple belonging to cultural groups. The construction

is a balance between security from the cultural "home" and the courage to seek new trails.

Folkestad (2002) takes care to distinguish between culture and ethnicity as related to MII. He explains cultural identity as a "bottom up" concept wherein cultural expressions such as music originate from popular forms that developed before the existence of our current national boundaries, or among people sharing the same musical interests regardless of national or ethnic affiliation. Ethnic identity combines both "bottom up" and "top-down" concepts in that ethnic identity can be interchangeable with the broader notions of nationality in one context, and associated with folklore and popular culture in other contexts. Ruud (1997, p. 165) further distinguished ethnic identity in music when he noted:

> Ethnicity is of course about cultural and personal intrinsic value, about identity and dignity. The music becomes an area on which one can present oneself and one's distinctive character in a positive way and by doing that reach respect for one's difference.

While music contributes to the identities of cultural and ethnic communities, it also contributes to youth identity development. In particular, popular music can serve as a "badge of identity" for many teenagers. Their musical behaviors are guided by both individual identity needs and group identity needs (Tarrant et al., 2002).

In terms of individual identity needs, music's appeal to adolescents may be based upon its ability to address several issues connected with adolescent development. These issues are associated with such tasks as acquiring a set of values and beliefs, performing socially responsible behavior, developing emotional independence from parents, and achieving mature relations with peers (Coleman, 1979; Kirchler et al., 1993; Palmonari et al., 1990). For example, many adolescents take note of the kinds and types of music their peers listen to when making decisions about whether they will pursue a friendship with someone (Tarrant, 1999; van Wel, 1994). Beyond being a means to evaluate others, teenagers' musical statements also help them to enhance their self-concept and self-image, particularly if the musical style with which they affiliate themselves is one approved of by their peers.

Social Identity Theory (SIT) provides one explanation for how music helps adolescents meet their social identity needs. SIT holds that a substantial portion of a person's self-concept is defined by his or her group memberships. Placing oneself squarely within the "in group" means that there are others who are excluded and become the "out group." When such group distinctions start to have meaning for adolescents, they begin to behave with regard to it and start to distinguish and discriminate between the "in group" and the "out group." Hypothetically, the extent of the discrimination is mediated by self-esteem: the less self-esteem an individual adolescent has, the greater is the motivation to discriminate. Successful discrimination enhances and/or restores self-esteem (Tarrant et al., 2002).

How "Personhood" Shapes Concepts of the Relationship of Music and Identity Development

Recently, Elliott and Silverman (2017) have proposed that any considerations of the role that music plays in the development of identity in all its facets (personal, cultural, social, gendered) must begin with the concept of personhood. Drawing from the work of several philosophers and scholars (e.g., Aristotle,1941; Bohlman, 2003; Dewey, 1929; Lieblich & Josselson, 2013;Van der Schyff, 2013) they argue that selfhood and personal identity are not the same as personhood but are primary dimensions of it.They define personhood as

> conscious self-awareness, self-identity, spirituality, and our powers of attention, perception, cognition, emotion, memory, and volition that emerge from, express, and develop because all dimensions of our personhood are unified and engage continuously with our socially situated communities, norms, and values.
>
> *(Elliott & Silverman, 2014, p. 63)*

Additionally, they describe the attributes of personhood as being grounded in the unified processes of body, brain, and mind, which, when combined with the awareness of one's connection to others, allows for the development of empathy, a critical facet of personhood.The following musical analogy provides an additional apt explanation of personhood:

> we propose that personhood is analogous to a huge jazz ensemble whose many millions of players—i.e., your embodied-enactive "personhood processes"—are so expert at improvising collaboratively with the dynamic circumstances of your human and natural ecosystems that the "beautiful music that is you"—which includes your conscious subjective life experiences, selfhood, self-efficacy, and spirituality—flow seamlessly and continuously from moment to moment. The "players" in your ensemble create your experience of you as the arranger and performer of your life's music.
>
> *(Elliott & Silverman, 2017, pp. 27–28)*

An important aspect of Elliott and Silverman's proposition of the significance of personhood as related to music and identity development is the idea that it is a process, and specifically, that the process of creating, performing, and responding to music is integral to the development of identity, whether it be Identity in

Music (IIM) or Music in Identity (MII). As Elliott and Silverman (2017, p. 32) have observed,

> each person's sense of musical identity—and other identities—is not isolated or fixed; it is contingent, fluid, and ever-changing, albeit imperceptibly at times. Our musical and personal identities change in relation to our musical and personal interactions, contexts, and the affordances that musical experiences provide.

These "musical affordances" are the tools or technologies that people use to develop and inform their identities. Elliott and Silverman propose that when we, as individuals, or as groups, come to identify with specific genres of music, or with specific ways of music-making (such as performing, composing, or responding), or with the people who make the music that we respond to emotionally, we are engaging in a process similar to what we do when we acknowledge the personhood in another. "[W]e make it true that a specific piece or musical-social event possesses the musical equivalent of personhood, in which case we, henceforth, embody and make that music part of our autobiographical personal-musical identities and selfhood" (Elliott & Silverman, 2017, p 40).

The ideas the Elliott and Silverman propose challenge the notion of music teaching as simply an act of transmitting information about music or developing music-making techniques. Their ideas suggest that the significance of music's role in the process of identity formation should be treated seriously and with "a conscious commitment to an 'ethic of care' and care-guided actions" (Elliott & Silverman, 2017, p. 43).

Gender Identity and Music

As we mentioned previously, in terms of culture and the development of musical identity (IIM), the perception of ourselves as "musicians" or of being "musical" is significantly affected by our social and cultural environment and by how we relate to others. Regarding music and the development of cultural and individual identity (MII), we noted that music is important in the establishment of identity within and across cultural communities. The characteristic of gender conflates or merges these two concepts of the relationship among music, culture, and identity.

Research on gender-related issues in music education has historically focused on attitudes about the propriety of specific music activities for cis-gender males and females, which often have been based on perceptions fostered by cultural standards and mores stemming from a given environment. Thus, expectations that learners may have for their own capacity to be successful in a variety of musical activities and endeavors may be regulated by their perceptions of what is a socially and culturally acceptable activity for cis-gender males and females and of the intersections between their own gender identity and their musical identity.

"[E]xpectations and hegemonic influences affect the developing musical identities of males and females differently" (MacDonald et al., 2011). For example, there has been considerable research examining differences in the types of instruments that boys and girls choose to learn to play and why (Abeles & Porter, 1978; Delzell & Leppla, 1992; Fortney et al., 1993; Griswold & Chroback, 1981; Harrison & O'Neill, 2000; MacLeod, 2009; O'Neill & Boulton, 1996; Sinsel et al., 1997; Tarnowski, 1993; Zervoudakes & Tanur, 1994). Almost invariably, the reasons for these choices are based upon cultural expectations of gender and or beliefs on the part of learners that specific musical instruments are inherently "masculine" or "feminine." Although research by Abeles (2009) suggests that these traditional gendered instrumental associations are shifting somewhat, other research (Wrape et al., 2014) suggests the opposite, indicating that gendered instrument stereotypes remain deep-rooted. When changes are noted, they are reflected primarily in an increase in the types and kinds of instruments that *girls* are choosing to play. Unfortunately, in comparison to females playing gender-atypical instruments, males who do so tend to be judged more harshly in terms of characteristics such as leadership and dominance (Conway, 2000; Taylor, 2009).

The "missing male" in vocal ensembles is another gender-related issue associated with musical identity development. Boys often enjoy singing from a very young age, but by the time they reach upper elementary age, they begin to view singing as an activity that is not appropriate for them. Even boys who continue to sing through the end of elementary school may find continued participation in vocal ensembles during middle school challenging because of the vocal change that accompanies adolescence. Freer (2010) suggested that boys' choices to avoid, decrease, or eliminate participation in choral music activities may be attributed to the theory of "possible selves." This theory posits that, more than any other group, adolescents (at least those in Western cultures), experiment with the notion of possible selves—the types of people they might become as adults. Freer further indicated that although adolescents have the capacity to hypothesize about possible selves, they have not yet necessarily mastered the skills needed to achieve those possible selves. This is frequently the case in music. If the opportunity to display competence is one motivation for adolescent boys to engage in an activity, then it is understandable that boys undergoing vocal change would consider avoiding an activity that places their vocal struggles on display.

In addition, the possible selves that adolescents think about may be positive or negative. According to Dunkel (cited in Freer, 2010, p. 23), "Adolescent boys spend significantly more time thinking about their negative possible selves than do females. This includes strategizing about how to avoid the realization of these negative possible selves." If that negative possible self is associated with involvement with a vocal ensemble (because they see the possible self of "choral musician" as predominantly feminine), then some male adolescents will try to distance themselves from that possible self.

Some of the gender-related issues in music that are specific to girls and women include identity challenges associated with puberty for girls, subtle deficit messages that may be inferred from studying a predominantly male-centered curriculum in school subjects, loss of opportunities in the choral program due to outnumbering boys by as much as three to one, and "the consequences of subjecting themselves to an activity where the societal and professional beliefs are that boys who sing are special, while girls who sing are ordinary" (O'Toole, 1998, p. 9).

These earlier studies paved the way for more recent investigations associated with music education and such human characteristics as attractional orientation and gender identity. In the case of these studies, the focus has been on the experiences in music education of teachers and students who identify with the LGBTQ+ community, as well as the extent to which the musical contributions of members of minoritized attractional orientations have been included or omitted from music education content and discourse.

An article written in 2000 by O'Toole for the *Bulletin of the Council for Research in Music Education* provided an early discussion of sexuality in the context of music education. One of O'Toole's main points was how sexual contexts can completely change conventional understandings of musics.

> Although queer theory has been accepted in many parts of the academy, our profession is not comfortable with discussions of sexuality and musicing, and actively silences identity positions based on sexuality ….With these sorts of institutional policies, gay teens who find their way into choirs are confronted by stifling politics and little support for emerging identities.
>
> *(O'Toole, 2000, pp. 36–37)*

The O'Toole article was one of very few published in music research journals during the time period regarding issues of attractional orientation and music education. and there had been no articles focusing on this topic in music education trade journals whose audience tended to be P-12 music educators. This changed in 2009, when Bergonzi's "Sexual Orientation and Music Education: Continuing a Tradition" was published in the *Music Educators Journal*. The article was groundbreaking in that it articulated for P-12 music practitioners the particular challenges faced by teachers and students who did not identify as heteroattractional. Moreover, Bergonzi placed squarely on the shoulders of the music education profession the responsibility to critically analyze the ways in which members of the LGBTQ+ community and the issues that concern them are made invisible.

> Isn't it time for us to acknowledge the ways we reinforce heterosexuality and the heterosexual lifestyle, and to examine how homophobia and heterocentrism bias our curricular content and the lives and work of LGBT music teachers? Isn't it time we eliminate heterosexuality's privileged place in our profession?
>
> *(Bergonzi, 2009, p. 26)*

Since 2010, there has been a manifold increase in articles and studies focused on music education and LGBTQ+ issues in general (Berman, 2017a; Garrett, 2012; Palkki & Caldwell, 2017; Rawlings & Espelage, 2020; Taylor, 2018; Taylor et al., 2020), attractional orientation (Berman, 2017b; Carter, 2013; Thomas-Durrell, 2020), and gender identity (Abramo, 2011; Aguirre, 2018; McBride & Palkki, 2020; Nichols, 2013, 2016; Palkki, 2015; Silveira, 2019; Silveira & Goff, 2016).

Throughout this section, we have identified a variety of ways in which socio-cultural factors mediate the development of the two types of musical identity: music in identity and identity in music. If it's true that children who engage intensely with music outside of the formal instructional environment of school are less likely to view themselves as "musical" or as "musicians," then the implications for music instruction are clear. Learners in our classrooms are in a constant state of identity development. If they are assured that the musical identities they are forming, whether individual or group identities, are valued and welcomed in the music classroom, they are more likely to view their musical experiences as meaningful and benefit positively from them.

Music Preference and Taste

Previously, we indicated that when learners are unable to find meaning in their learning, and when what they already know about a specific subject is not valued by their teachers or by the school, they become unmotivated and disengaged from learning. We also know that learners engage with music in a variety of ways outside of the classroom, and that engagement increases particularly during adolescence. What researchers have discovered about students' music preferences can be helpful to teachers interested in having a better understanding of what musical experiences will engage learners, balancing exposure to the familiar with providing a "Doorway-In(to)" (Wiggins, 2015) new musical discoveries.

We tend to be motivated to learn about music that we are interested in or music that we like. This tendency has led some researchers to develop theoretical models to explain human response to music, including how music preference decisions are made (LeBlanc, 1982) and music preference response (Hargreaves et al., 2005).

LeBlanc's model (see Figure 3.1) has a hierarchical structure of eight levels of variables influencing listening preference decisions. The model begins at Level 8, where input variables are identified, and moves upward in a progressive decision-making process until Level 1 is reached, the level in which the final preference decision is made.

LeBlanc speculated that children's music preference decisions were "based upon the interaction of input information and the characteristics of the listener, with input information consisting of the musical stimulus and the listener's cultural

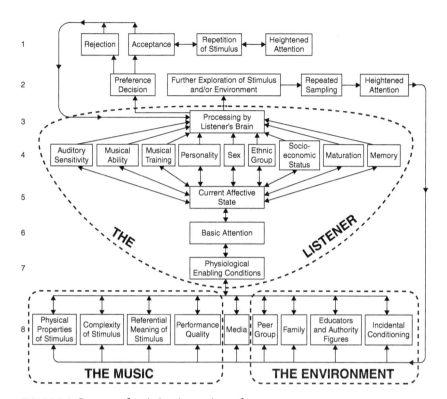

FIGURE 3.1 Sources of variation in music preference
Source: Fig. 7.1 from "The Development of Music Preference in Children" by A. LeBlanc, 1987. In J. C. Peer, I. W. Peery, & T. W. Draper (Eds.), *Music and Child Development* (pp. 137–157). New York: Springer. With kind permission of Springer Nature.

environment" (1982, p. 29). He classified media as another source of input information, in that the media "sample information from both the musical and the environment and present it to the listener for processing" (1982, p. 31).

As one way to test the viability of his model to explain factors that influence our musical preferences, LeBlanc (1988) investigated the components of the model from a sociological perspective: that is, how culture impacts or interacts with us in our music preference decisions. He surmised that the listener and the media function indirectly as culture. The environment functions directly as culture through the influence of affiliation groups (the family and the listener's peer group), agents representing societal institutions (such as educators and authority figures), and incidental conditioning (where the music choices of those who are part of the cultural environment are presented to the listener in settings that may have pleasant or unpleasant associations).

Not only does each of the elements of cultural activity function individually to influence music preference decisions, but they also function together in powerful ways. Four statements summarize how this overall effect of culture acts upon those who create and listen to music.

1. The culture provides a model for the appreciation of the music that it favors.
2. The culture rewards individual conformity with its own views about the value of different styles of music.
3. The culture greatly influences selection of the music people hear.
4. The culture influences the style of music created in the near future (LeBlanc,1988, p. 40).

To explain the phenomenon of preference and musical taste, Hargreaves et al. (2005) developed a "reciprocal feedback" model. The model was designed to demonstrate how the characteristics of three different components of a listening situation interact to generate a preference response and which may contribute to long-term patterns of musical taste. The three components that the researchers identified are the *person/listener* (e.g., age, gender, cultural group, musical training), the *music* (e.g., structure, style, complexity, familiarity), and the *listening context or situation* (e.g., work, leisure entertainment contexts; the presence or absence of others). They chose the term "reciprocal feedback" to acknowledge that each of the three components "can exert a simultaneous influence upon each of the other two, and because these mutual influences are bidirectional in each case" (Hargreaves et al., 2006, p. 136). The components identified by Hargreaves et al. are like those described in LeBlanc's (1982) model. In particular, the listener and the listening context components of this model seem to parallel LeBlanc's listener characteristics and the listener's cultural environment. Hargreaves et al. (2006, pp. 137–138) noted that the reciprocal feedback relationship between situations and contexts and the listener refers to "the interaction between the effects of music on a listener in a specific situation, and the ways in which individuals in contemporary society use music as a resource, for example in managing emotional states or moods."

Hargreaves (2012) proposed a revision of the original reciprocal-feedback model as an illustration of musical processing rather than musical communication (see Figure 3.2). As in the original model, the revised model contained the "music" and "situations and contexts" factors; however, the "listener" factor was revised to include "composer," "improviser," and "performer." In addition, he uses the term "musical imagination" to describe the type of cognitive activity foundational to musical production (i.e., performance) and musical perception (i.e., aesthetic preferences and psychological, cognitive, and affective responses).

The theoretical models developed by LeBlanc (1982) and Hargreaves (2012) help us to better understand how sociocultural factors mediate the components of the listener and the environment/listener context or situation to influence preference response, preference decisions, and the development of long-term

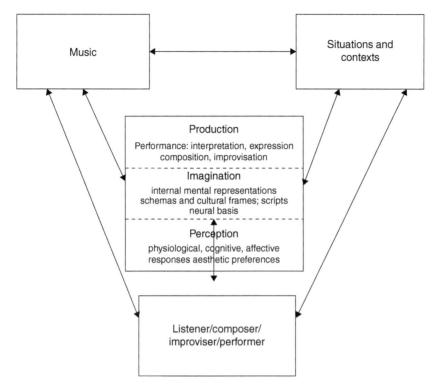

FIGURE 3.2 Revised reciprocal-feedback model of musical response
Source: From "Musical Imagination: Perception and Production, Beauty and Creativity" by D.J. Hargreaves, 2012. In *Psychology of Music, 40*(5). By permission of Sage Publications.

musical taste. While exposing learners to new and unfamiliar genres and styles of music is a function of music education, clearly, understanding learners' music preferences is important to increasing the motivation and interest of students, as well as maintaining the relevancy of music in school curricula.

Summary

Rather than being a process of simply acquiring knowledge and understanding, cognition involves changes that occur in all areas of cognitive processing because of our experiences with others as we build on the cultural practices and traditions of our cultural communities. Specific facets of culture such as social engagement and communication are important to cognitive development, and account both for variations in the definition of intelligence across cultures and considerations of variance in the methods and modes of knowledge construction among different cultural communities.

Extensive aural experiences are central to the process of cognition in music and lead to greater musical understanding. While we, as music educators, are responsible for helping them to be able to understand and decode standard and devised musical notation, we also must be careful that we do not unintentionally create barriers to that greater understanding by requiring students to read standard notation before they are ready or by devaluing the role that aural learning plays in the music-making of many cultures.

Like cognition, identity development is a complex process that results from the synthesis of multiple inputs associated with facets of the "self" and our sense of our own and others' personhood. Music not only contributes to our individual identity development (IIM), but our musical identities are an essential aspect of our social identity (MII) and, in both cases, culture plays a significant role. Additionally, gender development represents a combination of IIM and MII, in that culturally based perceptions related to gender and gender roles affect both our musical and social identities.

The styles and genres of music that learners prefer and the reasons for these preferences represent another aspect of who our learners are that must be considered in the music classroom. Often, before we endeavor to expose students to music that is new and unfamiliar, we must create a bridge to that new learning by starting with the music that they already know and appreciate.

We have a responsibility to recognize that most of our learners have vibrant and significant musical lives beyond the four walls of the music classroom or the ensemble rehearsal room, and that the ways they learn in the environments beyond school are often non-formal and highly motivational. We can invite learners to share that life within the music classroom, which means that as music educators, we must enlarge our vision of what music teaching and learning can be. If we take the time to learn about our students and understand the developmental processes and sets of experiences that have formulated who they are and how they see themselves, we can connect with them as learners in the music classroom in new and increasingly effective ways.

Questions for Discussion

1. Why do you think biology and culture were viewed for so long as separate entities in the human development process?
2. How would considering the connection between biology and culture make you think differently about the nature of human development?
3. Can you think of examples in your own experience in school where some of the information that formed your musical knowledge base was not valued or accepted?
4. What are some of the benefits to developing strong aural skills before attempting to read standard music notation?

5. How might having strong aural skills assist in learning to read music notation? Once one learns to read notation, is aural learning no longer necessary or valuable?

6. How does music contribute to your sense of individual identity? How would you describe your musical identity?

7. How might we as music teachers support all students including those who identify as part of the LGBTQ+ community?

8. How might you use some of the information regarding music preference to enhance learners' music experiences in your instructional environment?

References

Abeles, H. (2009). Are musical instrument gender associations changing? *Journal of Research in Music Education, 57*(2), 127–139. http:/doi.org/10.1177/0022429409335878

Abeles, H. F., & Porter, S.Y. (1978). The sex-stereotyping of musical instruments. *Journal of Research in Music Education, 26*(2), 65–75.

Abramo, J. M. (2011). Queering informal pedagogy: Sexuality and popular music in school. *Music Education Research, 13*(4), 465–477.

Aguirre, R. (2018). Finding the trans voice: A review of the literature on accommodating transgender singers. *UPDATE: Applications of Research in Music Education, 37*(1), 36–41. http://doi.org/10.1177/8755123318772561

Anderson, L. W., & Krathwohl, D. R. (Eds.) (2001). *A taxonomy for learning, teaching, and assessing: A revision of Bloom's taxonomy of educational objectives.* Longman.

Aristotle. (1941). *Basic works of Aristotle.* R. McKeon (Ed.). Random House.

Baumeister, R. F. (2005). Self-concept, self-esteem, and identity. In V. J. Derlega, B. A. Winstead, & W. H. Jones (Eds.), *Personality: Contemporary theory and research* (3rd ed., pp. 246–280). Cengage.

Bergonzi, L. (2009). Sexual orientation and music education: Continuing a tradition. *Music Educators Journal, 96*(2), 21–25.

Berman, A. S. (2017a). Creating an LGBTQ-friendly music program. *Teaching Music, 24*(3), 34–39.

Berman, A. S. (2017b). Honoring individuality: Perspectives on being a closeted, gay high school music educator. *Teaching Music, 25*(1), 56.

Bohlman, P. (2003). Music and culture: Historiographies of disjuncture. In M. Clayton, T. Herbert, & R. Middleton (Eds.), *The cultural study of music* (pp. 45–56). Routledge.

Bourdieu, P. (1986). The forms of capital. In J. Richardson (Ed.), *Handbook of theory and research for the sociology of education* (pp. 241–258). Greenwood.

Butler, A., Lind, V. R., & McKoy, C. L. (2007). Equity and access in music education: Conceptualizing culture as barriers to and supports for music learning. *Music Education Research, 9*(2), 241–253.

Byrd, C. M. (2016). Does culturally relevant teaching work? An examination from student perspectives. *SAGE Open, 6*(3), 1–10.

Carter, B. A. (2013). "Nothing better or worse than being Black, gay, and in the band": A qualitative examination of gay undergraduates participating in historically Black college or university marching bands. *Journal of Research in Music Education, 61*(1), 26–43.

Chavous, T. M., Bernat, D. H., Schmeelk-Cone, K., Caldwell, C. H., Kohn-Wood, L., & Zimmerman, M. A. (2003). Racial identity and academic attainment among African American adolescents. *Child Development, 74*(4), 1076–1090.

Cole, M. (1990). Cognitive development and formal schooling: The evidence from cross-cultural research. In L. C. Moll (Ed.), *Vygotsky and education: Instructional implications and applications of sociohistorical psychology* (pp. 89–110). Cambridge University Press.

Cole, M., & Scribner, S. (1977). Cross-cultural studies of memory and cognition. In R. V. Kail, Jr. & K. W. Hagen (Eds.), *Perspectives on the development of memory and cognition* (pp. 239–271). Erlbaum.

Cole, M., Gay, J., Glick, J. A., & Sharp, D. W. (1971). *The cultural context of learning and thinking.* Basic Books.

Coleman, J. C. (1979). *The school years.* Methuen.

Conway, C. (2000). Gender and musical instrument choice: A phenomenological investigation. *Bulletin of the Council for Research in Music Education, 146,* 1–17. http://doi.org/10.2307/40319030

Cook, N. (1998). *Music: A very short introduction.* Oxford University Press.

Correa-Chávez, M., & Rogoff, B. (2005). Cultural research has transformed our ideas of cognitive development. *International Journal of Behavioral Development, 29*(1), 7–10.

Delzell, J. K., & Leppla, D. A. (1992). Gender association of musical instruments and preferences of fourth-grade students for selected instruments. *Journal of Research in Music Education, 40*(2), 93–103.

Dewey, J. (1929). *Experience and nature.* Norton.

Elliott, D., & Silverman, M. (2014). Music, personhood, and eudaimonia: Implications for educative and ethical music education. *The Journal for Transdisciplinary Research in Southern Africa, 10*(2), 57–72. http://doi.org/10.4102/td.v10i2.99

Elliott, D., & Silverman, M. (2017). Identities and musics: Reclaiming personhood. In R. MacDonald, D. J. Hargreaves, & D. Miel (Eds.), *Handbook of musical identities* (pp. 27–45). Oxford University Press.

Folkestad, G. (2002). National identity and music. In R. MacDonald, D. Hargreaves, & D. Miell (Eds.), *Musical identities* (pp. 151–162). Oxford University Press.

Fortney, P. M., Boyle, J. D., & DeCarbo, N. J. (1993). A study of middle school band students' instrument choices. *Journal of Research in Music Education, 41*(1), 28–39.

Freer, P. K. (2010). Two decades of research on possible selves and the "missing males" problem in choral music. *International Journal of Music Education, 28*(1), 17–30. http://search.ebscohost.com/login.aspx?direct=true&db=eric&AN=EJ874561&site=ehost-live

Frith, S. (1996). Music and identity. In S. Hall & P. du Gay (Eds.), *Questions of cultural identity* (pp. 108–127). Sage. http://faculty.georgetown.edu/irvinem/theory/Frith-Music-and-Identity-1996.pdf

Fuligni, A. J., Witkow, M., & Garcia, C. (2005). Ethnic identity and the academic adjustment of adolescents from Mexican, Chinese, and European backgrounds. *Developmental Psychology, 41*(5), 799–811.

Garrett, M. L. (2012). The LGBTQ component of 21st-century music teacher training: Strategies for inclusion from the research literature. *UPDATE: Applications of Research in Music Education, 31*(1), 55–62. http://doi.org/10.1177/8755123312458294

Gauvain, M., & Munro, R. L. (2012). Cultural change, human activity, and cognitive development. *Human Development, 55*(4), 205–228.

Goodnow, J. J. (1976). The nature of intelligent behavior: Questions raised by cross-cultural studies. In L. B. Resnick (Ed.), *The nature of intelligence* (pp. 169–184). Erlbaum.

Gordon, E. E. (1999). All about audiation and music aptitudes. *Music Educators Journal, 86*(2), 41–44. http://doi.org/10.2307/3399589

Green, L. (2002). *How popular musicians learn.* Ashgate.

Griswold, P. A., & Chroback, D. A. (1981). Sex-role associations of music instruments and occupations by gender and major. *Journal of Research in Music Education, 29*(1), 57–62.

Gutierrez, K. D., & Rogoff, B. (2003). Cultural ways of learning: Individual traits or repertoires of practice. *Educational Researcher, 32*(5), 19–25.

Hargreaves, D. J. (2012). Musical imagination: Perception and production, beauty, and creativity. *Psychology of Music, 40*(5), 539–557.

Hargreaves, D. J., Miell, D. E., & MacDonald, R. A. R. (2005). How do people communicate using music? In D. E. Miell, R. A. R. MacDonald, & D. J. Hargreaves (Eds.), *Musical communication* (pp. 1–25). Oxford University Press.

Hargreaves, D. J., North, A. C., Tarrant, M., & McPherson, G. E. (2006). Musical preference and taste in childhood and adolescence. In G. McPherson (Ed.), *The child as musician: A handbook of musical development* (pp. 135–154). Oxford University Press.

Harrison, A. C., & O'Neill, S. (2000). Children's gender-typed preferences for musical instruments: An intervention study. *Psychology of Music, 28*(1), 81–97.

Jeffrey, P. (1992). *Re-envisioning past musical cultures: Ethnomusicology in the study of Gregorian chant.* University of Chicago Press.

Kirchler, E., Palmonari, A., & Pombeni, M. L. (1993). Developmental tasks and adolescents' relationships with their family. In S. Jackson & H. Rodriguez-Tomé (Eds.), *Adolescence and its social world* (pp. 145–167). Erlbaum.

Kohl, H. (1991). *I won't learn from you: The role of assent in education.* Milkweed Editions.

Lamont, A. (2002). Musical identities and the school environment. In R. MacDonald, D. Hargreaves, & D. Miell (Eds.), *Musical identities* (pp. 41–59). Oxford University Press.

LeBlanc, A. (1982). An interactive theory of music preference. *Journal of Music Therapy, 79*(1), 28–45.

LeBlanc, A. (1987). The development of music preference in children. In J. C. Peer, I. W. Peery, & T. W. Draper (Eds.), *Music and child development* (pp. 137–157). Springer-Verlag.

LeBlanc, A. (1988). The culture as educator: Elements in the development of individual music preference. In J. T. Gates (Ed.), *Music education in the United States: Contemporary issues* (pp. 33–43). University of Alabama Press.

Lieberman, D. A. (1997). Culture, problem solving, and pedagogical style. In L. A. Samovar & R. E. Porter (Eds.), *Intercultural communication: A reader* (8th ed., pp. 151–156). Allyn & Bacon.

Lieblich, A., & Josselson, R. (2013). Identity and narrative as root metaphors of personhood. In J. Martin & M. Bickhard (Eds.), *The psychology of personhood: philosophical, historical, social-developmental, and narrative perspectives* (pp. 203–222). Cambridge University Press.

Lilliestam, L. (1996). On playing by ear. *Popular Music, 15*(2), 195–216.

MacDonald, R., Hargreaves, D., & Miell, D. (Eds.). (2002). *Musical identities.* Oxford University Press.

MacDonald, R., Hargreaves, D., & Miell, D. (2011). Musical identities. In S. Hallam, I. Cross, & M. Thaut (Eds.), *Oxford handbook of music psychology* (pp. 462–470). Oxford University Press.

MacLeod, R. B. (2009). A comparison of aural and visual instrument preferences of third and fifth-grade students. *Bulletin of the Council for Research in Music Education, 179*, 33–43.

Marlowe, B., & Page, M. (1999). Making the most of the classroom mosaic: A constructivist perspective. *Multicultural Education, 6*(4), 19–21.

McBride, N. R., & Palkki, J. (2020). Big boys don't cry (or sing) … still? A modern exploration of gender, misogyny, and homophobia in college choral methods texts. *Music Education Research, 22*(4), 408–420.

McKoy, C. L. (2009). Cross-cultural competence of student teachers in music education. In S. Cooper (Ed.), *The Journal of the Desert Skies Symposium on Research in Music Education 2009 Proceedings* (pp. 128–144). University of Arizona.

Mills, J., & McPherson, G. E. (2006). Musical literacy. In G. E. McPherson (Ed.), *The child as musician: A handbook of musical development* (pp. 155–171). Oxford University Press.

Mistry, J. (2013). Integration of culture and biology in human development. *Advances in Child Development and Behavior, 45*, 287–314.

Nichols, J. (2013). Rie's story, Ryan's journey: Music in the life of a transgender student. *Journal of Research in Music Education, 61*(3), 262–279. http://doi.org/10.1177/00224 29413498259

Nichols, J. (2016). Sharing the stage. *Journal of Research in Music Education, 63*(4), 439–454. http://doi.org/10.1177/0022429415617745

O'Neill, S. A., & Boulton, M. J. (1996). Boys' and girls' preferences for musical instruments: A function of gender? *Psychology of Music, 24*(2), 171–183.

O'Toole, P. (1998). A missing chapter from choral methods books: How choirs neglect girls. *Choral Journal, 39*(5), 9–32.

O'Toole, P. (2000). Music matters: Why I don't feel included in these musics or matters. *Bulletin of the Council for Research in Music Education, 144*, 28–39.

Oyserman, D., Harrison, K., & Bybee, D. (2001). Can racial identity be promotive of academic efficacy? *International Journal of Behavioral Development, 25*(4), 379–385.

Palkki, J. (2015). Gender trouble: males, adolescence, and masculinity in the choral context. *Choral Journal, 56*(4), 24–35.

Palkki, J., & Caldwell, P. (2017). "We are often invisible": A survey on safe space for LGBT students in secondary school choral programs. *Research Studies in Music Education, 40*(1), 28–49. https://doi-org.libproxy.uncg.edu/10.1177/1321103X17734973

Palmonari, A., Pombeni, M. L., & Kirchler, E. (1990). Adolescents and their peer groups: A study on the significance of peers, social categorization processes and coping with developmental tasks. *Social Behavior, 5*(1), 33–48.

Perreira, K. M., Fuligni, A., & Potochnick, S. (2010). Fitting in: The roles of social acceptance and discrimination in shaping the academic motivations of Latino youth in the U.S. southeast. *Journal of Social Issues, 66*(1), 131–153. https://libproxy.uncg.edu/login?url= http://search.ebscohost.com/login.aspx?direct=true&db=a9h&AN=48465602&

Rawlings, J. R., & Espelage, D. L. (2020). Middle school music ensemble participation, homophobic name-calling, and mental health. *Youth and Society, 52*(7), 1238–1258.

Rogoff, B. (1981). Schooling and the development of cognitive skills. In H. C. Triandis & A. Heron (Eds.), *Handbook of cross-cultural psychology* (Vol. 4, pp. 233–294). Allyn & Bacon.

Rogoff, B. (2003). *Cultural nature of human development.* Oxford University Press.

Rogoff, B., & Angelillo, C. (2002). Investigating the coordinated functioning of multifaceted cultural practices in human development. *Human Development, 45*(4), 211–225.

Rogoff, B., Andrew D., Coppens, A. D., Alcalá, L., Aceves-Azuara, I., Ruvalcaba, O., López, A., & Dayton, A. (2017). Noticing learners' strengths through cultural research. *Perspectives on Psychological Science, 12*(5), 876–888.

Rosado-May, F. J., Urrieta, L., Dayton, A., Rogoff, B. (2020). Innovation as a key feature of indigenous ways of knowing. In N. S. Nasir, C. D. Lee, R. Pea, & M. McKinney de Royston (Eds.), *Handbook of the cultural foundations of learning* (pp. 80–96). Routledge.

Rummens, J. (2001). *An interdisciplinary overview of Canadian research on identity*. http://canada.metropolis.net/EVENTS/ethnocultural/publications/identity_e.pdf

Ruud, E. (1997). *Musikk og identitet* [Music and Identity]. Universitetsforlaget.

Scribner, S. (1974). Developmental aspects of categorized recall in a West African society. *Cognitive Psychology, 6*(4), 475–494.

Serpell, R. (1979). How specific are perceptual skills? A cross-cultural study of pattern reproduction. *British Journal of Psychology, 70*(3), 365–380.

Silveira, J. M. (2019). Perspectives of a transgender music education student. *Journal of Research in Music Education, 66*(4), 428–448. http://doi.org/10.1177/0022429418800467

Silveira, J. M., & Goff, S. C. (2016). Music teachers' attitudes toward transgender students and supportive school practices. *Journal of Research in Music Education, 64*(2), 138–158. http://doi.org/10.1177/0022429416647048

Sinsel, T. J., Dixon, W. E., & Blades-Zeller, E. (1997). Psychological sex-type and preferences for musical instruments in fourth and fifth graders. *Journal of Research in Music Education, 45*(3), 390–401.

Tarnowski, S. M. (1993). Gender bias and musical instrument preference. *Update: Applications of Research in Music Education, 21*(1), 14–21.

Tarrant, M. (1999). *Music and social development in adolescence.* Doctoral dissertation, University of Leicester.

Tarrant, M., North, A. C., & Hargreaves, D. J. (2002). Youth identity and music. In R. MacDonald, D. J. Hargreaves, & D. Miell (Eds.), *Musical identities* (pp. 134–150). Oxford University Press.

Taylor, D. (2018). Dignity for all: LGBTQ students and empathic teaching. *UPDATE: Applications of Research in Music Education, 36*(3), 55–58. http://doi.org/10.1177/8755123318761914

Taylor, D. M., Talbot, B. C., & Holmes, E. J. (2020). Experiences of LGBTQ+ students in music education programs across Texas. *Journal of Music Teacher Education, 30*(1), 11–23. https://doi.org/10.1177/1057083720935610

Taylor, M. D. (2009). *The relationship between music attitude and selected factors in elementary music students.* Doctoral dissertation, University of South Carolina.

Thomas-Durrell, L. (2020). Being your "true self": The experiences of two gay music educators who teach in the Bible belt. *Music Education Research, 22*(1), 20–41. http://doi.org/10.1080/14613808.2019.1703921.

Thorsen, S. (2002). Addressing cultural identity in music education. *Talking Drum, 84*, 18–21.

Van der Schyff, D. (2013). *Music, meaning and the embodied mind: Towards an enactive approach to music cognition.* MA thesis, University of Sheffield.

van Wel, F. (1994). A cultural gap between the generations? Social influences on youth cultural style. *International Journal of Adolescence and Youth, 4*(3–4), 211–228.

Villegas, A. M., & Lucas, T. (2002). *Educating culturally responsive teachers: A coherent approach.* State University of New York Press.

Villegas, A. M., Strom, K., & Lucas, T. (2012). Closing the racial/ethnic gap between students of color and their teachers: An elusive goal. *Equity and Excellence in Education, 45*(2), 283–301.

Vygotsky, L. (1978). *Mind in society: The development of higher psychological processes.* Harvard University Press.

Wagner, D. A., & Spratt, J. E. (1987). Cognitive consequences of contrasting pedagogies: The effects of Quranic preschooling in Morocco. *Child Development, 58*(5), 1207–1219.

Watson-Gegeo, K. L. (1990). The social transfer of cognitive skills in Kwara'ae. *Newsletter of the Laboratory of Comparative Human Cognition, 12,* 86–90.

Wiggins, J. (2015). *Teaching for musical understanding.* Oxford University Press.

Woody, R. H. (2012). Playing by ear: Foundation or frill? *Music Educators Journal, 99*(2), 82–88. http://doi.org/10.1177/0027432112459199

Wrape, E. R., Ditloff, A. L., & Callahan, J. L. (2014). Gender and musical instrument stereotypes in middle school children: Have trends changed? *Update: Applications of Research in Music Education, 34*(3), 40–47.

Zervoudakes, J., & Tanur, J. M. (1994). Gender and musical instruments: Winds of change? *Journal of Research in Music Education, 42*(1), 58–67.

4

THE INTERSECTION WHERE
TEACHING AND LEARNING MEET

A warm, safe, and caring environment allows students to influence the
nature of the activities they undertake, engage seriously in their study, regu-
late their behavior, and know of the explicit criteria and high expectations
of what they are to achieve.

Queensland, Australia Department of Education

*At the intersection where teaching and learning meet, we find a complex system of multiple
environments that either support or hinder culturally responsive teaching. In this chapter, we
explore the impact of certain dimensions of the classroom, school, and community environments on music learning. The chapter concludes with questions for discussion. Strategies for
creating and fostering culturally responsive environments in our classrooms, schools and communities are explored in Chapters 5–7.*

The Classroom Environment

Learning occurs in a complex social and cultural system involving peers, teachers,
parents, and community members. How and what a child learns is affected by
a myriad of factors and is dependent not only on individual characteristics, but
also on environmental influences. Urie Bronfenbrenner (1979), an early pioneer
in ecological theory (or bio-ecological theory), proposed that everything around
us impacts how we develop as human beings. Bronfenbrenner divided a person's
environment into five systems: the microsystem, the mesosystem, the exosystem,
the macrosystem, and the chronosystem.

The microsystem, described as the closest and most influential environment to
the child, refers to those people the child encounters on a daily basis. Children

DOI: 10.4324/9781003208136-6

have direct contact with people in the microsystem and relationships are bi-directional. The microsystem usually includes home and school. Surrounding the microsystem is the mesosystem, which references the cross-relationships among significant people in a child's life. For example, how a parent interacts with the teacher will have an effect on what and how a child learns. When different areas of the microsystem are working together, there is a positive impact on a child's development. Likewise, when members of the microsystem are working against each other, the child may be negatively impacted. The third system, the exosystem, is made up of people who do not have direct contact with the child but are indirectly involved in the child's development. Friends of the family, school administrators, and parents' employers are part of this middle system. The fourth system, the macrosystem, refers to the prevailing culture and economic conditions of society. Changes and shifts that occur over time are associated with the fifth system, the chronosystem. Adapting the work of Urie Bronfenbrenner (1979), and drawing upon the construct of culturally responsive teaching, we propose that learning is impacted by the classroom environment, the school environment, the community, and the larger society (see Figure 4.1).

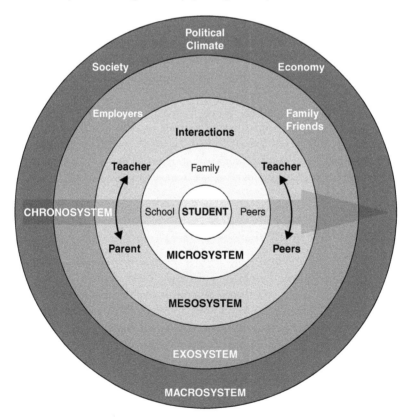

FIGURE 4.1 Illustration of ecological theory

You will notice in Figure 4.1 teachers and peers are members of the system closest to the learner and are identified as highly influential in child development. Students spend a large part of their day in the classroom and most of their face-to-face (bi-directional) encounters with peers and teachers occur in the classroom. The interactions among teachers and students (mesosystem) result in a unique classroom environment that has been shown to impact several dimensions of student learning and development. Research finds that when the classroom environment reflects a caring, nurturing environment, student academic performance and sense of belonging improves. Unfortunately, when students feel like the outsider, or when they sense others think of them as a problem to be solved, they may develop feelings of frustration, anger, and unworthiness that can result in poor attendance, low achievement, behavioral problems, and leaving school (Davis, 2017; Muñiz, 2019).

Much of this chapter focuses on the relationship between classroom environment and student achievement; yet the link to motivation is an important one for music teachers. Motivation is not only tied to academic success but also plays a role in music participation. Although most PreK–5 schools offer music to all students, in grades 6–12 music instruction is often an elective. If students are not motivated to study music, they simply opt out. Understanding motivation and student participation is vitally important if we want to provide equal access to all students, particularly in light of a disturbing pattern that has surfaced over the past several decades. Although we have witnessed a rapid increase in the number of students of color enrolled in schools (Aud et al., 2013), there tends to be a disproportionately low number of students from racial and ethnic minorities participating in music. The words spoken by the former president of the Music Educators National Conference, Charles Hoffer, in 1988 still ring true today:

> In my travels around the United States as President of the Music Educators National Conference, I have the leisure of hearing many outstanding performing groups, including a number of all-state groups. These organizations represent the finest performers in a particular school or state … Casual observation of these fine performing groups reveals a disturbing fact: minority students are not represented in anywhere near the numbers one would expect … If music education is for all students, which has been one of its stated goals for over fifty years, then the small number of minority students is a matter of concern—and action.
>
> *(Hoffer, 1988, p. 5)*

There are a multitude of factors influencing the enrollment of students in the racial/ethnic minority in music including school funding, community support, and family expectations, but student motivation certainly plays a role. In one of my first research projects, I (Vicki) investigated the impact of the classroom environment on enrollment in music ensembles of students from racial and ethnic minority groups (Lind, 1999). I used the Classroom Environment Scale (CES) developed by Trickett and Moos (1995) to investigate the relationship between race/ethnicity and music participation. I found Hispanic students were less likely to be involved in music programs that were perceived as competitive (defined by how much students had to compete for grades and/or recognition) or in programs connected to teachers who were perceived as overly controlling (defined as particularly strict with frequent and severe punishment). In a later study investigating African American student participation, enrollment in music was also associated with these elements of the classroom environment (Lind & Butler, 2003).

Creating Supportive Classrooms

The relationship between teachers and students is a critical factor in establishing a supportive environment, and creating a supportive environment that is conducive to learning is critical to culturally responsive teaching. Teachers wanting to create supportive classroom environments must first and foremost demonstrate they care for their students. In addition, teachers must have high expectations for their students' academic success, and they must be willing to work hard to help students succeed (Gay, 2018; Howard, 2020; Ladson-Billings, 1995, 2021; Paris, 2012). All students need to know their teachers have their best interests at heart. According to Gay (2018, p. 46):

> [T]eachers who really care for students honor their humanity, hold them in high esteem, expect high performance from them, and use strategies to fulfill their expectations. They also model academic, social, personal, and moral behaviors and values for students to emulate. Students, in kind, feel obligated to be worthy of being so honored. They rise to the occasions by producing high levels of performance of many different kinds—academic, social, moral, and cultural.

Culturally Responsive Caring

Teachers who incorporate the type of caring identified as integral to culturally responsive teaching do not view any of their students through a deficit lens where cultures that differ from the dominant norm are perceived as inferior. Rather, such teachers hold affirming views of students from diverse cultural backgrounds, seeing cultural diversity as an instructional asset and resource for learning rather than a problem to be solved or an inconvenience to be tolerated (McCallops et al., 2019; Villegas & Lucas, 2002).

Culturally responsive caring goes beyond just the feelings we have towards our students; it is connected to action. Teachers who demonstrate culturally responsive caring are concerned about the whole child and take responsibility for nurturing both academic success and psychological well-being. Gay (2018, p. 59) described caring as a major pillar of culturally responsive teaching, "manifested in the form of teacher attitudes, expectations, and behaviors about students' human value, intellectual capability, and performance responsibilities." Teachers who exhibit this type of caring are persistent; they continually look for ways to connect with their students. They recognize and value individual differences and work to find multiple ways of working with students. Ayers (2004, p. 11) described caring teachers as those who "assume a deep capacity in students, an intelligence (often obscure, sometimes buried), as well as a wide range of hopes, dreams, and aspirations" and who create an environment that has "multiple pathways to success."

Music educators are in a unique position to demonstrate cultural caring with students because we often teach the same students over the course of several years. Elementary-aged students will typically have the same music teacher for six years, (PreK–5). In situations where music teachers serve both a high school and the middle school that "feeds" into the high school, they may have the same students for three to seven years, depending on whether the students remain in a music program throughout middle and high school. Having the opportunity to work with the same students over time not only allows music teachers to develop deeper relationships with their students but may also help teachers develop culturally affirming perspectives.

Culturally responsive caring requires many of us (particularly those of us who attended small, suburban or rural schools) to rethink what caring looks and sounds like in the classroom. I (Vicki) grew up in a small town in western Kansas. One of my favorite teachers was my fourth-grade teacher, Mrs. Springs. I can remember her soft-spoken demeanor and generous hugs. I remember sitting in class enraptured by the sound of her voice as she read to us. I also remember straight rows and quiet hallways. I always sat in the front row, and I usually raised my hand before talking. On those occasions when a friend sitting nearby distracted me, Mrs. Springs would simply ask if everything was alright, and I would return my attention to the task at hand. In my mind, the warm hugs and quiet voice reflected a caring teacher.

I still remember the stark contrast when I first walked into a large urban school outside of Los Angeles 20 years later. I found the tone of voice used by many of the teachers and administrators disturbing. I had never heard such brutal honesty, and such strong voices. I quickly learned, however, that the teachers in the school truly cared about their students. Their voices were not reflecting anger but rather reflected a deeply felt urgency for student success.

Understanding Communication Styles

Writing about classroom management in urban education, Brown (2004) explained that some students enrolled in schools in urban settings might be used to a more direct form of communication than students from rural or suburban settings. According to Porter and Samovar (1991, p. 21), culture influences "what we talk about; how we talk about it; what we see, attend to, or ignore; how we think; and what we think about." Gay (2018) indicated that ethnic communication styles represent fundamental traits of group tendencies. It is important to note that individual members of a group may exhibit communication characteristics that vary in specific ways from the group. Although overgeneralizing should be avoided, attention to these tendencies is imperative in optimizing the possibility for effective communication across cultures. Gay further notes, "Culturally responsive teacher preparation programs teach how the communication styles of different ethnic groups reflect cultural values and shape learning behaviors and how to modify classroom interactions to better accommodate them" (Gay, 2002, p. 111).

Traditional school settings emphasize linear thinking. For many of us, this is how we learned, and it seems natural to teach our students to communicate in a similar fashion. However, the communication styles that are often valued in the classroom, and which tend to be influenced by middle-class values of appropriate discourse in instruction, may not be the styles familiar to or commonly used by learners. For example, one approach to communication, which Gay (2018) refers to as "topic-chaining," involves weaving together a variety of issues and ideas into a single story. This often results in students including much more background information and using a more indirect approach than some of us are used to. Unfortunately, teachers often underestimate the abilities of students who have a different way of communicating. When students communicate using a style that is highly contextual and that is more conversational, it may come across as rambling and disjointed. In addition, students' perceptions of how their ways of communicating are received in the classroom impact how they learn as well as their attitudes about learning.

Understanding the differences in cultural communication styles allows teachers to better understand their students' abilities and to design instruction to meet diverse needs. While learning the types and styles of discourse specific to an academic discipline is certainly an important instructional objective, learners' culturally situated styles of communication must also be valued and respected. These two outcomes need not be mutually exclusive in the classroom environment.

Communication also plays an important role in classroom management. Clear communication can set students up for success by explicitly outlining expectations for academic success and classroom behavior. Novice teachers in particular, sometimes have trouble clearly stating their expectations and speaking with authority

(Brown, 2004). Whether it is because they lack experience or because they feel timid and out of place, it is not uncommon for young teachers to stumble over their words or have trouble expressing exactly what it is they want from their students. Delpit (2006, p. 135) pointed out this may create specific problems for students who experience a more direct form of communication at home.

> One of the most difficult tasks we face as human beings is trying to communicate across our individual differences, trying to make sure that what we say to someone is interpreted the way we intend. This becomes even more difficult when we attempt to communicate across social differences, gender, race, or class lines, or any situation of unequal power.

I (Vicki) observed a White, 28-year-old, male student teacher work with a first-year level SSA choir. The young women who were enrolled in the choir were predominantly African American. The student teacher asked the choir if they wanted to stand and join him for warm-ups. A few students moved to the risers while others remained seated. There was quite a bit of verbal sparring back and forth among the students and the teacher as he tried to get all the students to agree to stand and sing. I could tell the student teacher was frustrated and he later told me that his feelings were hurt because the students acted up in front of me. He thought the students were being disrespectful and he was not sure what to do. I pointed out that he had given the students a choice by the way he phrased his instruction. Those students who remained in their seats and answered with a resounding "no" were simply responding to his question honestly.

There was certainly a cultural disconnect between the teacher and the students in the women's choir. The pre-service teacher was particularly uncomfortable when the students began speaking over his instructions (even though he had technically asked them a question and they were responding to that question). I did not, however, interpret the students' responses as disrespectful. Instead, I recognized it as a style of interaction that I have observed in numerous classrooms.

Gay (2002) explained that some African American students use a call–response interactive communication style where the roles of speaker and listener are "fluid and interchangeable" (p. 111). The students use this style of communication to express their feelings about what the teacher is saying. The response is not meant to disrupt but is a way of participating in the conversation.

The significance of communication in creating a supportive music classroom environment relates not only to verbal and non-verbal (gestural) communications between teachers and students, but to musical expression as well. Being aware of the differing aesthetic value systems that shape what people view as significant and important in their music can assist music teachers in understanding what their students may be trying to communicate musically. Many music teacher preparation programs focus almost exclusively on music from the Western European classical and art music traditions. The aesthetic value systems operating within these musical traditions are often very different from those that function within the music of other macro- and micro-cultures of the world. In the context of school music, students who do not feel they can communicate musically or verbally with their teachers may feel marginalized and disengage from music instruction and from music programs. Hoffman (2011, p. 34) observed:

> Students who come from cultural backgrounds different from the pre-dominantly White, Christian cultures that influence our music teaching profession may experience frustration in the music classroom. Not surprising, their ways of learning and knowing music can appear to conflict, and therefore cause frustration, with traditional music pedagogies. Beyond these temporary misunderstandings, we may lose the ability to reach many students.

In the book, *Culturally Responsive Choral Music Education: What Teachers Can Learn from Nine Students' Experiences in Three Choirs*, Shaw (2020) vividly described how the disconnect between traditional choral music education and the lived musical experiences of her students required her to rethink traditional choral pedagogy. After having a student comment that he did not want to "sing like no White girl," and later talk about dropping out of the choir because they were not singing music the student valued, Shaw began to question what she had learned about choral music education in her university studies.

> All I had learned about choral pedagogy was gleaned in university environments where experiences focused primarily on the Western classical tradition of choral singing, a tradition I continue to value and teach. During my early teaching career, the way I had initially learned to teach choir appeared on the surface to be compatible with the needs of my learners, the majority of whom were White, middle class, and residing in suburban communities. Yet comfortable and familiar ways of teaching seemed not to serve my students in Chicago, who were predominantly pupils of color, equally well. This is not to say that pupils of color, in general, wouldn't identify with the Western classical tradition or desire to learn it, but that my specific singers at that time considered different musical styles and genres to be more relevant to their experiences.
>
> *(Shaw, 2020, p. 2)*

Music teachers who recognize and value the vast store of knowledge and skills that students already possess are less likely to belittle or invalidate the music that is an integral part of their students' musical lives.

The Value of High Expectations

There is a great deal of conversation in education about the need for teachers to maintain high expectations for all students. This conversation has been generated by a concern that, too often, teachers do not have the same high expectations for the academic achievement of students from racial and ethnic minority groups as they do for other learners. Having high expectations for all students means that teachers must be able to see the bigger picture of future possibilities that their students may not yet be able to envision.

Growing up in a southern community in North Carolina, I (Connie) attended an elementary school where the school population and the teachers were all African American. Even though the *Brown* court decision had been handed down only a few years earlier, *de facto* segregation was still in evidence. Like many children, I had some teachers in my school whom I adored and some that I tolerated. There was an experience I had as a child with one of the teachers who fit the latter category which, at the time, I viewed as very negative. This teacher was preparing our third-grade class for a school assembly where we would be reciting verses from the Bible. My teacher was adamant about our enunciating our words to a point that I thought was beyond extreme.

> An—**D** the earth was withou—**T** for—**M**, an—**D** voi—**D**, an—**D** dar—**K**—ness was upo—**N** the face of the dee—**P**! *Actors on television don't talk like this*, I thought. *It sounds so fake!*

I hated every moment that I had to spend practicing for the assembly and drew a huge sigh of relief when it was finally over. Now, as an adult, I realize that the exercise that I had viewed as fake and ridiculous was a significant act of caring on the part of my teacher based on her understanding of the time period in which I and my peers were growing up. No doubt she surmised that the world beyond our classroom would not have very high expectations of us as Black children. Though her methods may have seemed severe, developing our ability to speak clearly, distinctly, and with poise was one of many tools she used to challenge and contradict the lowered expectations of the larger society.

In his explanation of effective instructional practices for culturally diverse students, Howard (2020) described observing rigorous and challenging coursework and interviewing teachers who refused to lower their expectations for students' learning. Effective teachers design instruction so that students are actively involved in work that is demanding and meaningful (Abrami et al., 2008; Darling-Hammond & Oakes, 2019; Howard, 2020). Unfortunately, not all teachers assume a deep capacity in students, particularly when there are cultural differences or when teachers are early in their careers. Ballantyne and Mills (2008) looked specifically at novice music teachers and found that many young teachers had a very narrow understanding of their students' ability and sometimes confused being "busy" with being actively engaged.

There are unique challenges facing music teachers who are working to design meaningful and demanding lessons for all students. Not only do our students come from diverse backgrounds with different learning styles, but many of our students have very different experiences in music. Students with several years of private instruction may be working alongside peers with little or no background in music study. In the Ballantyne and Mills' study mentioned earlier, a young teacher described how she worked with diverse learners:

> They don't all have to be on the one sort of instrument. It can be a more simplified instrument for some of the lower ability kids so they can still be involved and take part. [For example] you get the upper-level kids to play a melody, you can get the lower level kids just to play the bass part, just to keep the beat, and it keeps them involved and they feel like they're accomplishing something as well.
>
> *(Ballantyne & Mills, 2008, p. 82)*

Certainly, this young teacher has worked to adapt the learning objectives based on her perception of individual needs, but the scenario hints at a potential problem. It is possible for music teachers to lower their expectations for student learning based on the prior experiences of the student. In fact, several teachers interviewed in the study talked about the need to "cater" to students from diverse backgrounds or with different learning styles. They described modifying classroom activities and expectations based on what they perceived as the needs of the students.

> One of the schools I've had to majorly change the way I teach because there's a lot of kids that are ESL and a lot of kids with behavior problems ... And I'm doing stuff that I've never done before ... just to suit those kids ... The ESL kids ... probably can't understand half of the things that I'm saying so ... [I use] written cards, or workbooks and stuff they can see, rather than just me telling them, to make it easier for them to understand it.
>
> *(Ballantyne & Mills, 2008, p. 83)*

These examples highlight two potential problems for music teachers working to individualize instruction. First, teachers may be reinforcing the discrepancies between the "haves" and the "have nots" by providing supplemental activities for advanced students who are engaged in private music study. Second, teachers may limit opportunities for certain students based on behavior rather than ability. The authors of the study point out these approaches to inclusivity have "the potential to alienate and re-emphasize existing inequalities in their classrooms" (Ballantyne & Mills, 2008, p. 83). In contrast, the culturally informed version of care is tied to expecting excellence from all students and demanding accountability when students do not live up to expectations (Howard, 2020). Robinson (2006, p. 45) illustrated this when describing Gina, a White general music teacher in a predominantly African American school.

> Bonding more closely with her students in no way changes the high expectations she has for them in the classroom and concert venue. Gina does not give her students permission to fail. I have seen her demonstrate for the students what an A, B, or C graded effort looks like in their classroom activity; I've also witnessed her stop during a choir selection in her spring concert to remind the students *who they were and where they were* and in the next moment helping them create beautiful music together.

Learning Communities

Working collaboratively to create beautiful music is the cornerstone of many music education programs. Students in choir, band, or orchestra programs work collaboratively, under the leadership of the director, to improve musical performance while learning about music and music-making. This setting is ideal for promoting democratic principles by fostering learning communities. Teachers who organize their classrooms as communities of learners foster a disposition of collaborative learning between and among students and create a positive teacher–learner relationship based on mutual respect (Ladson-Billings, 1995). Building a learning community among diverse learners means understanding how to design communal learning environments that benefit a variety of learning styles, and which enable learners to see themselves as having knowledge that can contribute to the learning process (Gay, 2018; Ladson-Billings, 1995; Villegas & Lucas, 2002).

Sharing responsibility and collectively making decisions that are best for the class reflects the democratic principles we hold in high esteem. To truly promote a democratic classroom, teachers must trust their students to be able to make good decisions and must give up some of their control to allow for student input. Brown (2004) pointed out that many urban youths lead challenging lives outside of school and carry heavy responsibilities. Many students help support their families financially and some are raising their own children. When we consider the decisions that these students must make daily, it should not surprise us that they want some control over the decisions being made about their education. By undervaluing our students' opinions, and by making unilateral decisions based on what we believe to be best for students, we again operate from a deficit model.

We know that students from low socioeconomic backgrounds and students of color tend to feel less "connected" to their schools than affluent or White students and this is, in part, because of the cultural disconnect and lack of autonomy. Brown (2004, p. 268) described the need to develop "a classroom social environment in which students agree to cooperate with teachers and fellow students in pursuit of academic growth." Creating such an environment is an ongoing process with teachers adjusting and adapting to the changing needs of their students. It requires teachers to respond to the emotional, social, and cognitive needs of the students. While classroom management is vital to culturally responsive teaching, there are certainly unique challenges facing many of today's teachers; we know that a "one-size-fits-all" approach simply will not work. Hymann and Snook (2000) suggest democratic classrooms that emphasize cooperation, mutual goal setting, and shared responsibility support greater student affiliation. Students are more engaged and are less likely to act out if they are a part of the process. In fact, the researchers state, "Students behave because it is the right thing to do and because they respect the rights of others" (Hymann and Snook, 2000, p. 495).

In addition, a democratic approach capitalizes on students' social skills and supports deeper learning through collaboration and shared responsibility (Gallavan, 2011). Adrienne, a teacher in an urban school interviewed as part of the study conducted by Brown in 2004, described conversation as a "primary priority" for her students. She further stated, "They are from very verbal environments. I find that they can handle side discussions and engage in the main discussion at the same time" (Brown, 2004, p. 281). Culturally responsive teachers facilitate learning by capitalizing on the need for human interaction; yet the principles of collaborative learning as they relate to culturally responsive teaching go much deeper than group projects or working within an ensemble for a shared purpose. The principles encompass both shared expertise and shared responsibility. Delpit (2006) described a classroom teacher in a high school where the student population was predominantly African American, who allowed her students to study rap songs. Working collaboratively, the students explained to the teacher the "rules of rap." The teacher then used what she learned from her students to build a lesson on the structure of grammar. By allowing students to take responsibility for the content of instruction (structure of rap) and by providing opportunities for the students to share their expertise, the teacher was able to connect prior knowledge to new content in a meaningful and memorable context.

The very nature of music study in K–12 classroom and rehearsal environments is characteristic of a learning community, particularly when students are engaged in musical performance. Every member is responsible for contributing to the whole that is the musical performance, and the attentive music teacher understands how to maximize the talents and potentials of each student in the cause of a meaningful and fulfilling performance. However, culturally responsive teaching requires that teachers broaden the scope of performance possibilities so that, in addition to being exposed to traditional Western European classical musical genres and ensembles, students have opportunities to engage with music in ways that are congruent with their own lived cultural experiences with music (Abril, 2009, 2013; Kelly-McHale, 2019; Kindall-Smith, 2006; Kruse, 2020; Mixon, 2009; Robinson, 2006; Shaw, 2020).

In music teacher education programs, learning communities that support culturally responsive pedagogical practices provide pre-service teachers opportunities to work together to construct understandings of music teaching and learning within multiple cultural contexts. In this way, the likelihood of students' equitable access to music is increased.

The Culture of the School

Members of the education system that have an indirect relationship with students (the exosystem) also impact learning and play an important role in how schools work with diversity. For example, administrators and teachers who are unfamiliar with a student's cultural background often misinterpret cultural differences as misbehavior. As a result, students of color are suspended from school more frequently, punished more severely, referred for special education services at a disproportionately higher rate, and feel less connected to their schools than their White counterparts (Battistich et al., 1995; Bazon et al., 2005; Losen, 2015; Losen et al., 2014; Miguel & Gargano, 2017). We contend this trend can be reversed if we better understand the cultural disconnect between some students and the school culture and then actively look for ways to bridge this disconnect.

One contributing factor to problems students from racial and ethnic minority groups face in school is what Valenzuela (2010) described as "subtractive schooling" where students' knowledge is actually treated as a deficit (see our discussion of the "deficit model" in Chapter 1). Frequently in music, certain types of music are disregarded or disparaged while other types are held in high esteem. Similarly, some schools with large immigrant populations downplay the value of the student's native language and promote an "English Only" model. It is not unusual for students to feel disconnected from a school when they do not see or hear their cultural background represented in the school hallways, lunchroom, or administrative offices. This is magnified when they are disciplined for behavior that reflects their family and cultural backgrounds.

A second factor that contributes to a cultural disconnect is what is often referred to as the "hidden curriculum" of schooling. Although most schools have written policies that describe dress codes, academic expectations, and rules for behavior, there are hidden norms associated with these aspects of schooling. How school rules are interpreted and enforced can vary widely among different school environments. If the expectations are not clearly articulated, and if they are not in line with prior experiences, students may feel alienated or targeted (Mehan et al., 1996).

There may be specific times when the shift between home and school is particularly difficult for some students. For example, a student who comes from a very verbal background may have a particularly hard time remembering to raise her hand to ask questions if she is returning to school after being at home for an extended length of time. Even the simple act of turning off a cell phone may be innocently overlooked on a day-to-day basis. Looking for patterns in behavior and helping students navigate the transition between home and school may require increased sensitivity on the part of teachers and administrators.

Family and Community Connections

Extended family and community members are often part of the exosystem and impact education. Unfortunately, much of the rhetoric in education paints a picture of dysfunctional families, crime-ridden neighborhoods, and drug-infested communities. As the immigrant population grows, we are also beginning to hear more about the cultural divide between non-Western families and school expectations. Certainly, these are challenging times for many communities. Our work, however, is guided by the fundamental belief that families and communities are sources of strength for our students and can be valuable contributors to student success.

Numerous educational scholars have pointed out that African American families come from a long line of strong African ancestors who have overcome tremendous obstacles, including slavery, discrimination, and segregation. Looking at families through a strength prospective allows us to recognize the contributions of Black families including a strong work orientation, the belief in family, and a strong orientation towards achievement (Brice & McLane-Davison, 2020; Hill, 1999). Many of our immigrant families have likewise demonstrated resilience in the face of physical, financial, psychological, and emotional hardships. Drawing upon rich histories and cultural traditions, we see a reflection of the values we often promote in schools such as strong work ethics and complex problem-solving. Additionally, families and communities reflect rich and vibrant music traditions. We will be better situated to provide for the needs of our students if we recognize and capitalize on the strengths of their families and community members.

Research indicates that many parents, including those from "mainstream" American families, feel inadequate when dealing with schools (Turnbull & Turnbull, 2001). Parents from diverse backgrounds or who are members of a racial/ethnic minority group often feel at an additional disadvantage because of the way they dress, the color of their skin, the sound of their voice, or the language they speak. In "A Challenge to Professionals: Developing Cultural Reciprocity with Culturally

Diverse Families," Maya Kalyanpur (2003) described the experiences of a Pakistani mother who wore a *shalwar-kameez*, the formal dress from her native country, to the first meeting at her daughter's school. She described being asked immediately if she spoke English and subsequently being treated in a condescending manner. She learned quickly to dress in Western clothing and present herself in a more "American" way for future meetings. Likewise, an Israeli mother described sending her American husband to initial school meetings to avoid any negative stereotypes that would manifest themselves as a result of her accent.

Immigrant parents are often viewed as outsiders, and they are often kept on the outside by the traditions and norms of the educational system. Knowing how schooling works and understanding how to navigate the system (referred to as cultural capital) is much easier for family and community members who experienced the system as children. The phrases we use, the abundant number of acronyms prevalent in education, and legal terminology can be overwhelming. Consider the story of a young Indian mother who described frequently needing clarification on the terms and phrases used in her daughter's school. "I felt stupid saying, 'Stop, I don't know what you're talking about,' and nobody took the time to explain. Ten years later, I still feel sometimes that I'm groping in the dark" (Kalyanpur, 2003, p. 2).

Politics and the American Educational System

Political, social, and economic conditions in America continue to play an important role in education. We often hear rhetoric about the need for education reform and a commitment to equity in education. We have witnessed numerous legislative efforts designed to improve schools including the *No Child Left Behind Act* (NCLB, 2002) and *Race to the Top* (U.S. Department of Education, 2009). Alongside changing legislation, we have also seen a shift towards school choice initiatives and, consequently, public funds are now used to support charter and private option schools. Despite these continued efforts to transform schools, we continue to see a gap in the opportunities and outcomes for many of our students. Too often, American education is neither just, nor fair (Howard, 2020).

Providing equitable access to high-quality music instruction has been a concern for many music educators over the past several decades. Based on the results of numerous research studies, we know that, unfortunately, not all students have the opportunity to participate in school music. While we can look at enrollment trends to identify where the disparity lies, we do not have a great deal of research looking specifically at cause and effect. Elpus and Abril (2011) found that twelfth-grade Spanish-speaking English language learners were half as likely to participate in music ensembles (band, orchestra, or choir) compared with peers. Their research found that White students were significantly overrepresented in music classes as were students from higher socioeconomic status backgrounds, native English speakers, students in the highest standardized test score quartiles, children of parents holding advanced postsecondary degrees, and students with GPAs ranging from 3.01 to 4.0. They hypothesized the disparity in enrollment was due to geographical differences, access to music classes, and/or cultural differences.

> The choice of enrolling in music during high school seems to be the result of a complex selection process—not yet fully understood—that leads to substantial population differences between students who do and do not elect music that are measurable prior to the commencement of music course work.
>
> *(Elpus, 2013, p. 178)*

Lorah, Sanders, and Morrison (2014) specifically investigated music participation rates among English language learners and reported findings similar to Elpus and Abril; however, Lorah et al. linked the disparity to socioeconomic status and academic achievement.

> The apparently lower representation of ELL students in music ensembles can be interpreted more accurately as an underrepresentation of students from poorer families and students experiencing lower academic achievement.
>
> *(Lorah et al., 2014, p. 240)*

Like Elpus and Abril, the authors described school site factors that might be serving as barriers to music participation for some students.

> in an effort to facilitate student learning in the core areas of literacy and numeracy, the addition of remedial support or "second-dose" classes to a student's schedule may limit severely or eliminate the possibility of a music elective. Likewise, the real or perceived cost of music participation may discourage participation among students with limited financial resources.
>
> *(Lorah et al., 2014, pp. 240–241)*

Elpus and Abril (2019) extended their previous 2011 work by examining the demographics profile of high school students enrolled in music ensembles during any of their four years, based on their transcripts as opposed to their self-reported responses to a questionnaire. Some results were like those found in their 2011 study (e.g., the overrepresentation in music ensembles of students who are White, of middle to high socioeconomic status, are native English speakers, and exhibit high academic performance). However, at least one finding contradicted their 2011 research results. Though they found that race was significantly associated with overall music ensemble enrollment, they also discovered that, regarding race or ethnicity, the demographic profile for students enrolled in choral ensembles was not significantly different from the general school population. They surmised several possible reasons for this outcome: (1) Opportunities for students to perform music from a variety of cultures and incorporate multiple performance techniques and practices may be attractive to students of varied backgrounds; (2) Students' access to choir does not necessarily require prior study; (3) Participation in choral ensembles may require less time commitment and fewer financial demands, which could be appealing to students with work or family responsibilities and limited financial resources. While this unexpected result is encouraging, the researchers suggested that additional research is necessary to more deeply investigate possible reasons for the results they uncovered and develop a greater understanding of how best to reach students.

Elpus also identified national educational policies as a barrier to equitable access to music education. For example, Elpus reported that the implementation of the *No Child Left Behind Act* "exacerbated the preexisting underrepresentation in music courses of Hispanic students, English language learners, and students with Individualized Education Plans" (2014, p. 215). Although his research was not designed to show cause and effect, Elpus made the following observation:

> The precise mechanism through which these students were excluded from music courses remains an open question. It is possible that school administrators, responding to consequential accountability pressures, systematically denied access to music courses for these subgroups in favor of courses more closely aligned with the high-stakes test.
>
> *(Elpus, 2014, p. 228)*

It is troubling to think about the structural barriers in place that limit our students' access to music education. It is even more troubling if those students who are banned from participating in school music are those who would have limited options for music study outside of the school environment. We acknowledge that limiting music and the arts was probably not the intended outcome of the legislation, and schools do not knowingly build structures that create a divide between who has and who does not have access to music instruction. Yet the reality is, these unintended barriers to music education exist and their existence exacerbates the inequality that is present in many schools across the country.

Summary

As Bronfenbrenner (1979) pointed out in his ecological theory, how students develop and learn is, in part, dependent upon the environment in which they live and learn, and upon their relationship with those around them. School environments that support learning for all, those that reflect culturally responsive caring, require consistent and persistent efforts by administration and faculty. By recognizing the strengths of the students in our classrooms and creating communities of learning based on shared leadership models, we can develop a system that encourages all students to engage in the learning process.

Bronfenbrenner's ecological theory also described how the relationships between the people who most closely surround a child have an impact on child development. In school, that means the relationships between the teachers and parents and the teacher and other students matter. Trusting relationships based on mutual respect can help foster a sense of belonging for both the adults and students, and these relationships can serve as a role model for what the classroom should look like. Unfortunately, for parents who did not have good experiences in school, the relationships can be strained. Finding ways to rebuild these relationships is imperative if we want to create supportive learning communities.

We acknowledge there are no easy answers to some of the issues posed in this chapter, but we believe that change is possible. Important strides have been made in our understanding of how the interactions among students, teachers, families, and society impact education. We are better able to create supportive school environments when we broaden our understanding of the cultural differences that exist in communication styles, concepts of caring, and motivation as it relates to music education. In Part II of this text, we will explore specific ways in which we can apply our understanding of culturally responsive teaching in music classrooms, schools, and communities to provide more equitable music education opportunities for all students.

Questions for Discussion

1. Who has been an influential person in your life and how did they shape your teaching?
2. Who are influential people in the lives of school-age children and what role do they play in education?
3. Which dimensions of the classroom environment are most closely affected by (a) the teacher, (b) by the administration, or (c) by families?
4. How can the classroom environment either hinder or support student learning?
5. How do you define *culturally responsive caring*? What are the attributes of a caring teacher?
6. How can differences in communication impact the classroom?
7. How does our political system influence music education directly and indirectly?
8. How has the current political climate impacted what you teach in your classroom?
9. What are strategies you can employ to develop a supportive and culturally responsive classroom environment?

References

Abrami, P. C., Bernard, R. M., Borokhovski, A. W., Surkes, M. A., Tamim, R., & Ahzng, D. (2008). Instructional interventions affecting critical thinking skills and dispositions: A stage one meta-analysis. *Review of Educational Research*, *78*(4), 1102–1134. http://doi.org/10.3102/0034654308326084

Abril, C. (2009). Responding to culture in the instrumental programme: A teacher's journey. *Music Education Research*, *11*(1), 77–91. http://doi.org/10.1080/14613800802699176

Abril, C. (2013). Toward a more culturally responsive general music classroom. *General Music Today*, *27*(1), 6–11. http://doi.org/10.1177/1048371313478946

Aud, S., Wilkinson-Flicker, S., Kristapovich, P., Rathbun, A., Wang, X., & Zhang, J. (2013). *The condition of education 2013* (NCES 2013-037). U.S. Department of Education, National Center for Education Statistics. http://nces.ed.gov/pubsearch

Ayers, W. (2004). *Teaching the personal and the political: Essays on hope and justice.* Teachers College Press.

Ballantyne, J., & Mills, C. (2008). Promoting socially just and inclusive music teacher education: exploring perceptions of early-career teachers. *Research Studies in Music Education*, *30*(1), 177–191. https://doi.org/10.1177/1321103X08089891

Battistich, V., Solomon, D., Kim, D., Watson, M., & Schaps, E. (1995). Schools as communities, poverty levels of student populations, and students' attitudes, motives and performance: A multilevel analysis. *American Educational Research Journal*, *32*(3), 627–658. https://doi.org/10.3102/00028312032003627

Bazon, B., Osher, D., & Fleischman, S. (2005). Research matters/creating culturally responsive schools. *Educational Leadership*, *63*(1), 83–84.

Brice, T. S., & McLane-Davison, D. (2020). The strength of Black families: The elusive ties of perspective and praxis in social work education. In A. N. Mendenhall & M. M. Carney (Eds). *Rooted in strengths: Celebrating the strengths perspective in social work* (pp. 25–38). University of Kansas.

Bronfenbrenner, U. (1979). *The ecology of human development: Experiments by nature and design.* Harvard University Press.

Brown, D. F. (2004). Urban teachers' professed classroom management strategies: Reflections on culturally responsive teaching. *Urban Education*, *39*(3), 266–289. https://doi.org/10.1177/0042085904263258

Darling-Hammond, L., & Oakes, J. (2019). *Preparing teachers for deeper learning.* Harvard Education Press.

Davis, J. R. (2017). From discipline to dynamic pedagogy: A re-conceptualization of classroom management. *Berkeley Review of Education*, *6*(2), 129–153.

Delpit, L. (2006). *Other people's children: Cultural conflict in the classroom.* The New Press.

Elpus, K. (2013). Is it the music or is it selection bias? A nationwide analysis of music and non- music students SAT scores. *Journal of Research in Music Education*, *61*(2), 175–194. https://doi.org/10.1177/0022429413485601

Elpus, K. (2014). Evaluating the effect of No Child Left Behind on U.S. music course enrollments. *Journal of Research in Music Education*, *62*(3), 215–233. https://doi.org/10.1177/0022429414530759

Elpus, K., & Abril, C. (2011). High school music ensemble students in the United States: A demographic profile. *Journal of Research in Music Education*, *59*(2), 128–145. https://doi.org/10.1177/0022429411405207

Elpus, K., & Abril, C. R. (2019). Who enrolls in high school music? A national profile of U.S. students, 2009–2013. *Journal of Research in Music Education*, *67*(3), 323–338.

Gallavan, N. (2011). *Navigating cultural competence in grades K–5: A compass for teachers.* Corwin Press.

Gay, G. (2002). Preparing for culturally responsive teaching. *Journal of Teacher Education, 53*(2), 106–116. https://doi.org/10.1177/0022487102053002003

Gay, G. (2018). *Culturally responsive teaching: Theory, research, and practice* (3rd ed.). Teachers College Press.

Hill, R. (1999). *The strengths of African American families: Twenty-five years later.* University Press of America.

Hoffer, C. (1988). Key issues and concerns: Black participation in music in higher education. *Center for Black Music Research Register, 1*(2), 5.

Hoffman, A. R. (2011). Do you hear what I'm sayin'? Overcoming miscommunications between music teachers and students. *Music Educators Journal, 97*(4), 33–36.

Howard, T. C. (2020). *Why race and culture matter in schools: Closing the achievement gap in America's classrooms* (2nd ed.). Teachers College Press.

Hymann, I., & Snook, P. (2000). Dangerous schools and what you can do about them. *Phi Delta Kappan, 81*(7), 488–501.

Kalyanpur, M. (2003). A challenge to professionals: Developing cultural reciprocity with culturally diverse families. *Focal Point, 17*(1), 1–6.

Kelly-McIale, J. (2019). Research-to-resource: Developing a culturally responsive mindset in elementary general music. *Update: Applications of Research in Music Education, 37*(2), 11–14. https://doi.org/10.1177/8755123318810111

Kindall-Smith, M. (2006). I plant my feet on higher ground: Music teacher education for urban schools. In C. Frierson-Campbell (Ed.), *Teaching music in the urban classroom II: A guide to leadership, teacher education, and reform* (pp. 47–66). Rowman & Littlefield.

Kruse, A. J. (2020). Rethinking the elementary "canon": Ideas, inspirations, and innovations from hip-hop. *Music Educators Journal, 107*(2), 58–65.

Ladson-Billings, G. (1995). Toward a theory of culturally relevant pedagogy. *American Education Research Journal, 32*(3), 465–491.

Ladson-Billings, G. (2021). I'm here for the hard re-set: Post pandemic pedagogy to preserve our culture. *Equity and Excellence in Education, 54*(1), 68–78.

Lind, V. R. (1999). Classroom environment and Hispanic enrollment in secondary choral music programs. *Contributions to Music Education, 26*(2), 64–77.

Lind, V. R., & Butler, A. (2003). African American enrollment in secondary choral music programs and the classroom environment. *The Phenomenon of Singing 4. Proceedings of the International Symposium,* St. John's, Newfoundland, Canada.

Lorah, J., Sanders, E., & Morrison, S. (2014). The relationship between English language learners' status and music ensemble participation. *Journal of Research in Music Education, 62*(3), 234–244.

Losen, D. J. (2015). *Closing the school discipline gap: Equitable remedies for excessive exclusion.* Teachers College Press.

Losen, D. J., Hodson, C., Ee, J., & Martinez, C. (2014). Disturbing inequities: Exploring the relationship between racial disparities in special education identification and discipline. *Journal of Applied Research on Children, 5*(2), 1–20.

McCallops, K., Barnes, T., Berte, I., Fenniman, J., Jones, I., Navon, R., & Nelson, M. (2019). Incorporating culturally responsive pedagogy within social-emotional learning interventions in urban schools: An international systemic review. *International Journal of Educational Research, 94*, 11–28.

Mehan, H., Villanueva, I., Hubbard, L., and Lintz, A. (1996). *Constructing school success.* Cambridge University Press.

Miguel, C., & Gargano, J. (2017). Moving beyond retribution: Alternatives to punishment in a society dominated by the school-to-prison pipeline. *Humanities, 6*(2), 15. https://doi.org/10.3390/h6020015

Mixon, K. (2009). Engaging and educating students with culturally responsive performing ensembles. *Music Educators Journal, 95*(4), 66–73.

Muñiz, J. (2019). *Culturally responsive teaching: A 50 state survey of teaching standards.* New America. www.newamerica.org

No Child Left Behind (NCLB) Act of 2001, Pub. L. No. 107-110, § 115, Stat. 1425 (2002).

Paris, D. (2012). Culturally sustaining pedagogy: A needed change in stance, terminology, and practice. *Educational Researcher, 41*(3), 93–97. https://doi.org/0.3102/0013189X12441244

Porter, R. E., & Samovar, L. A. (1991). Basic principles of intercultural communication. In L. A. Samovar & R. E. Porter (Eds.), *Intercultural communication: A reader* (6th ed., pp. 5–22). Wadsworth.

Robinson, K. (2006). White teachers, student of color: Culturally responsive pedagogy for elementary general music in communities of color. In C. Frierson-Campbell (Ed.), *Teaching music in the urban classroom: A guide to survival, success, and reform* (pp. 35–53). Rowman & Littlefield.

Shaw, J. T. (2020). *Culturally responsive choral music education: What teachers can learn from nine students' experiences in three choirs.* Routledge.

Trickett, E. J., & Moos, R. H. (1995). *Classroom environment scale.* Consulting Psychologists Press.

Turnbull, A. P., & Turnbull, H. R. (2001). *Families, professionals, and exceptionality: Collaborating for empowerment* (4th ed.). Merrill.

U.S. Department of Education. (2009). *Race to the Top: Executive summary.* www2.ed.gov/programs/racetothetop/executive-summary.pdf

Valenzuela, A. (2010). *Subtractive schooling: U.S.-Mexican youth and the politics of caring.* State University of New York Press.

Villegas, A. M., & Lucas, T. (2002). Preparing culturally responsive teachers: Rethinking the curriculum. *Journal of Teacher Education, 53*(1), 20–32.

PART II
Application

5

APPLICATIONS IN THE CLASSROOM

I believe that teachers learn just like students learn. I believe that students tell you what they need to know.

Leonora, elementary general music teacher

Chapter 5 begins our section on Application and focuses on ways to transform the music classroom into a culturally responsive setting through an exploration of what that setting might look like, sound like, and feel like. Through the use of vignettes and comments from pre- and in-service music educators and administrators who use culturally responsive teaching practices in their own classrooms and schools, we will demonstrate the practical application of the principles and concepts of culturally responsive teaching introduced in the first part of the book.

Culturally Responsive Teaching in Action

What does culturally responsive teaching look like in a music classroom? This is the question we seek to address in this chapter. In the first part of this book, we indicated that culturally responsive teaching is more than an approach to instruction; it is a disposition—a mindset. Teaching music in a way that is responsive to the culturally based musical knowledge, strengths, skills, and interests students bring to the music learning process requires specific intent. In addition, culturally responsive teaching requires understandings that are multifaceted.

The vignettes, reflective prompts, and strategies that follow are all designed to help the reader envision culturally responsive teaching in action and to provide a framework for reflective practice. The vignettes have been written to illustrate specific aspects of culturally responsive teaching. These vignettes have been

DOI: 10.4324/9781003208136-8

inspired by the stories we have heard from numerous music students, teachers, and administrators, and by our own experiences in the classroom. The vignettes do not represent a single event or describe a specific person. Rather, they are an amalgamation of events and people from across the country. We have also included direct quotes from people we interviewed for this book. The interviewees included K–12 music educators, university professors, undergraduate and graduate music education students, and an administrator. We consciously sought out people from different racial and ethnic backgrounds and from different regions across the country and we interviewed people with different levels of experience and expertise regarding culturally responsive teaching.

With one exception, we have used pseudonyms to protect the identities of those who agreed to let us use their words. Their stories provide a context for the foundational information presented in Part I, and their words enrich in meaningful ways the ideas for incorporating culturally responsive teaching in the classroom. We must caution, however, that it is not our intent to be prescriptive in offering these examples. There are no "tips and tricks" to providing instruction in music that is culturally responsive. As with other examples of good pedagogical practice, employing culturally responsive teaching effectively in the music classroom takes knowledge, understanding, commitment, and patience.

Getting to Know Yourself

Vignette

Jeff grew up in a large family with three younger brothers, two sisters, and numerous cousins. As the oldest child in the family, Jeff often took care of his younger siblings. He loved his family and he loved working with young children. In fifth grade, Jeff was introduced to the band world, and he was immediately drawn to the trumpet. He became an accomplished musician, and after graduating from high school was accepted into the music education program at the state university.

Jeff excelled in music education; the faculty members appreciated his work ethic and his understanding of working with young children, and his classmates frequently sought him out for assistance. He was a natural when assignments included teaching episodes and his student teaching experience was a complete success. His mentor teacher wrote a glowing recommendation letter upon his graduation and Jeff was quickly hired to teach at a nearby elementary school.

Jeff's first few weeks went well, and he felt confident that he was going to have a great year. Jeff had planned his curriculum for the year, and he intended to use music that "all" children knew to teach the elements of music. Jeff, however, found himself struggling as the year continued. The students did not know the songs he intended to use in class, and they did not seem to like most of them. Jeff was a member of a Facebook group for elementary teachers, so he posed a question asking if others had noticed that students did not seem to know common nursery rhymes or standard children's songs. The responses were a mixed bag, but some posts shocked Jeff. Some teachers seemed genuinely angry at society because they were not teaching "American" songs or because not all students came into the classroom knowing the same stories and folk tunes. Jeff began to think about the music he had selected and the reasons he chose what he did.

Reflective prompt: Think about the music you listened to as a child, what you heard in your home and what was part of the world around you. Was that music part of your school experience? Were you ever made to feel that your "home" music had less value than the music you listened to in class?

In Their Own Words: Perspectives on Music Education

In Chapter 2, we indicated that the development of cultural competence was a critical factor in learning to teach in a culturally responsive way. We also said that to develop cultural competence, teachers must get to know themselves. That is, they must critically reflect on how their lived experiences, values, beliefs, and biases (both explicit and implicit) affect how they choose to approach their students and the music curriculum.

Typically, teachers have tended to take a stance of racial neutrality regarding their students in an effort to demonstrate impartiality. Unfortunately, the insistence on "not seeing race" implies that to see racial differences is to acknowledge a deficit among racially minoritized groups. Claire teaches strings in an elementary arts magnet school. Her description of how she used to view her students is an example of this tendency.

> I came in (and I know you've probably heard people say this) with this whole notion of "I don't see difference" when I come into the classroom. "I don't see race. Everybody's the same." (God, what an idiot!). I mean, you know, it's not true. You know, if you have a child that doesn't have the means from home, and don't assume that they all don't—you know, I have children here whose parents are college professors, I have other children who walk to school, I mean it's everybody, it's everything. So, you can't make any assumptions about anything.

Several of the people we interviewed mentioned that their interest in and commitment to culturally responsive teaching began from reflecting on their own cultural experiences. Lena, a teacher with Latin American ancestry, discussed how she came to realize not only the impact of her own cultural background on how she experienced music but also the importance of teachers acknowledging culture in their classrooms.

> *My grandfather immigrated from Chile when he was a young man and encountered a lot of racism and xenophobia but loved music and persisted in that and shared that with me and my sisters … His wife, my grandmother, was a language professor and so her home was always full of people from everywhere, and so it was expected as part of my childhood, that we would be listening and learning and valuing people's stories, even if they were not the same as our own, especially if they were not the same as our own. And then, as I got older, I realized how much of my grandfather's* Latinidad, *as we say, was in how I experienced music and how I move and how I talk and the social norms I expect as a Latina, in terms of social knowledge construction, touch in a class-room, expectations for warmth. And then my marriage was to a Japanese American man who immigrated when he was five … and graciously shared [early memories of school] with me. So … there are just so many compelling stories of why it matters for how a kid feels in class and then how they take that home with them and how that impacts how they grow up. And so, for me, my ethnically and culturally and linguistic-ally diverse students are top priority, not just because of my ideals, but because of my family story.*

Luis, who teaches elementary general music in an International Charter School shared that his interest in culturally responsive teaching was born out of his experiences growing up in a community where, as Filipino immigrants, he and his family were in the ethnic minority.

> *I grew up in upstate New York, where it was 95% White and the only people of color that I knew were my family and my three good friends, so we knew we were different. As a kid I would bring fried fish and rice to school and then the kids would be like, "oh that's weird" and then I would change it, and I would try to become what the social norm is for that area and maybe like America. So, as a teacher now, how I feel teaching in a culturally responsive way is important to me is that it keeps the integrity of what makes, in my opinion, America, America. We all come from different places, different backgrounds … and we say that we celebrate that, and we should, so we shouldn't be bringing stigmas and making people feel uncomfortable with sharing what makes their family unique or what they like or anything like that.*

Another important outcome of teachers engaging in critical self-reflection is that the teacher can serve as a model, showing a willingness to be vulnerable and thus encouraging students to be vulnerable as well. As Stew, a master's student in music education observed:

> *I think that we can't ask our students to be vulnerable and … really dive into their culture with the teacher and the students without exhibiting that vulnerability. Why should they be open to you if you can't be open with them? I think it's important to look at your own culture, look at your own privilege and see where your roots are. See how you can incorporate your own culture into the classroom, and hopefully modeling that behavior you can create a culture of vulnerability and a culture where students see it's safe to express maybe hidden parts of themselves. I think the more open you can be with your students and the more open they can be with you, the more meaningful learning experiences you can incorporate into the classroom.*

For other interviewees, new self-awareness regarding explicit and implicit biases was gained while reading materials introduced in school- and district-wide professional development. Claire described what happened when she read a book on diversity for a class she was taking and served on a team of teachers presenting the book to her school faculty.

> *And the first thing the book said was that our society is all about race. I thought "No, it's not!" I was going through my house stomping, talking to God about it, like "No, it's not! It's not all about race!" It suddenly dawned on me, it's because you're White, Claire! You don't know what it's like to walk into a room where you're the only person of color, you don't understand what it feels like … I think that in saying that we don't see color, we're trying to say that we're going to be fair to everybody, but if you're going to be fair to everybody, you need to understand everybody.*

All our interviewees' statements support the importance of engaging in critical self-reflection as a part of the process of developing cultural competence. Before teachers can really understand their students, they must understand their own assumptions and critically reflect on how their assumptions impact their teaching.

Strategies for Getting to Know Yourself

To engage in critical self-reflection and self-assessment, consider asking yourself the following questions:

- Do I view cultural differences from a deficit perspective or from a perspective that neutralizes culture in an effort to "be fair"?
- Is my instruction biased toward mainstream ways of learning?
- Do I view students who follow mainstream classroom practices as being more highly motivated and achieving than students whose ways of behaving and learning are culturally different?
- Do I make assumptions about ethnic/cultural groups or underrepresented populations based on stereotypes or implicit bias?

Getting to Know Your Students

Vignette

Mr. Barker believes that the best way to teach the students in his general music class is to connect with them, and the best way to connect with them is to learn about them. He starts every school year with an activity based on a circle activity he learned from Janet Barrett (Campbell et al., 2021) at a professional development workshop. For this activity, students are given a blank sheet of paper and asked to create a diagram of their musical history by drawing circles to show different music activities in their personal background. Students may include any categories they wish but are given a few examples such as early childhood memories, songs you hear in the car, favorite songs, songs heard at home, or songs learned in school. Students are then encouraged to list songs or short descriptions of music that fits in each of the categories. By getting to know about the students' musical backgrounds, Mr. Barker learns about family histories and traditions, and is able to draw upon the students' prior experiences as he plans for music learning.

Since Mr. Barker does not live in the community where he teaches, he encourages his students to let him know when they are involved in special musical events in the community and he tries to attend as often as he can. He gets to see many of his students in a different context, which gives him a more complete picture of who they are musically, so that he can plan more effectively to help them achieve their own musical goals.

Reflective prompt: What challenges might you face when trying to get to know a community other than the one you are a member of? How might you overcome these challenges?

In Their Own Words: Perspectives on Music Education

Cultural competence in the classroom requires that we get to know our students, learn about their goals and aspirations, and understand what they bring to the classroom. The importance of knowing your students was a recurring theme throughout our interviews. As an administrator, Jill understood the impact that teachers' knowing their students can have on building a learning community.

> *When the teacher invites the students to listen to music as a part of the opening of a class and the teacher intentionally selects world music without preempting the kids, "OK, today we're going to listen to an Afro Cuban …" No, just play it and then letting the kids connect to it and share how they connected. The craziest stories come out and I don't mean crazy, I just mean unexpected because it is so easy to assume that kid's culture*

must be … because they look like … that kid's culture must be … because they sound like … and the teachers will say, "well, like I didn't know that" and it's knowing the kids but hearing it from the kids and so inviting them. I think that my teachers feel that that they are the most responsive when they know the kids and they know the kids best when they put lots of things out there on the table for the kids to react to.

Lena discussed why knowing her students was foundational to her work as a music educator.

I think about my students and the first thing I see is their faces. And I think about how the arc of my year and then my presence in class and the way I receive and work with them in class needs to reflect not just materials that would connect with their home cultures or pedagogy that would support anti-racism for Black and Brown students but what am I really doing beyond instructional strategies and beyond materials to connect with the ways students from racially ethnically and culturally linguistically diverse backgrounds are constructing knowledge, are experiencing music, are experiencing me, are experiencing each other, and how can I change my autopilot White norms from the University and my own upbringing so that they get to be the most musical that they can be in class?.

Lloyd has seen first-hand the advantages of getting to know his students by observing their response to a new colleague.

That's it [getting to know your students]. That's the whole game. That is the name of the game. That really has to be what we are about. I have a new assistant director this year. He just finished his master's degree. This is his first teaching job; he's a little older, about 25 or 26. He is hilariously funny and the kids just flock to him. He really does take it on to make this his personal mission. He goes to their soccer games; he goes to see their theatrical performances. He's taking a couple kids to a performance this weekend. He's all about trying to get to know kids and plug into their interests.

Learning about our students' cultural background is likewise an important step in developing cultural competence. All of us, including our students, are a reflection of the experiences we have inside and outside of the classroom; we cannot really begin to know our students if we only focus on who they are *as* students. John believes that having conversations with his students helps him to get to know who his students are in meaningful ways, and he uses what he learns to inform his curricular choices.

I find informal conversations really important. When I talk informally with a student about what they did over the weekend, I find out a lot about what their family's musical world is. Also, asking the families. When I sign up kids for chorus, there is a spot that says—on the back of this sheet—just give me a snapshot of your family's musical world. It's very interesting. Sometimes I use that to inform repertoire. More [often] than not, I use it to just have a sense of knowing who my students are and where their strengths lie, what they are familiar with and where I can stretch them.

Audrey echoed John's belief that it was important to get to know the students and understand that each student is unique. She stressed that getting to know her students on an individual basis was one of the most important aspects of her job as a teacher.

You have to know who your kids are and where they come from and know what they are experiencing and what it might be like at home and what they are going through. You really just have to know your kids. It's not just like teaching a pile of kids who all care and understand and have good behavior. It's about teaching kids who might have a tough time at home and that's why they aren't responding to you today … It's knowing your kids and what their backgrounds are and what they are going through so you can best approach each kid.

Stew provided a student's point of view and stressed how important it is to get to know your students as individuals.

In terms of my teachers—they didn't really utilize many culturally responsive peda-gogical practices in the classroom. I feel they didn't really see the need for it because they were teaching to a bunch of rich White kids, which is not an excuse for not being culturally responsive. I had an interesting conversation with one of my colleagues about culturally responsive pedagogy and how people sweep the culture of White kids under the rug. Everyone wasn't just born in America. Everyone has ancestry and culture that extend hundreds of years back. Really looking at and acknowledging the culture that exists within each and every one of your students, not just the non-White students—even in a classroom of all rich White kids, you can absolutely implement culturally responsive practices.

Stew went on to describe how he wanted his teachers to acknowledge his heri-tage and bring things into the classroom that would help him learn about his own family's histories.

Learning about our students can be particularly critical for students who are refugees to the United States. For them, the initial adjustment to a new school can be challenging and confusing and, in some cases, can understandably interfere with their capacity to learn and flourish. Jill is the principal in a high school known for its proactive approach to the sociocultural diversity of its student population. She shared what her school has done to mediate the challenges that students who are refugees face when enrolling in a new school.

We kept doing these focus groups with students, particularly undocumented students and refugees, because we just felt like we weren't reaching them and what we learned from just having either translators or us speaking with them directly in their language was that we weren't "on boarding" the kids very well. So, they've just come from a refugee camp and now they're in America and they're happy to be here, and the caseworker drops them off at the school … "Yeah, see you. Get on the bus this afternoon." And we would give them the schedule, but we weren't helping them understand what it means to be an American student.

And so, we started recruiting international student ambassadors who are there to meet the student when they get there. There's a map of the world and the kids can see, "Oh look, there's other kids in here from where I am." Or "Wow, I can't wait to meet those students from that other place" and it just shifted the kids' perceptions from "I have to fight to make my way in here" to "They're easing my way into this." That shift as an administrative team has just permeated into everything we do with kids.

Allen told a vivid story that emphasized the importance of learning about our students. His story illustrates how important it is for teachers to consider their students' worldview and recognize that different students interpret classroom interactions differently, depending upon their backgrounds and lived experiences.

In my first views of teaching, I was taught never to touch students. And then I had a Latino student say to me one day "You don't even like us." And I'm like "What are you talking about?" He said, "You never touch us … if you say, 'good job,' you never pat us on the shoulder or do anything like that." And I was left going, "What do you mean?" And then suddenly, you know, I started to ask them, and they're like, "Yeah well, our [Mexican] teachers, if we did a good job, they would at least pat us on the shoulder or give us a hug." Now, "Oh my God!" I never even considered something like that, especially when you're raised in an educational environment, when you're taught constantly don't touch your students under any circumstances. So at that point I started getting into the habit, if the student was doing a good job or if a student needed a hug (you're just very conscious of the lines, where they were), I would, I wouldn't hug my Anglo students unless they were expressly clear it was OK, but my Latino students, generally, if you pat them on the shoulder, it meant a great deal more than saying "good job." "Good job" was just words; but a pat on the shoulder was being culturally responsive to what they needed for their success.

As noted in Chapter 3, our students' self-concept is often intricately connected to the music they identify with. For many of our students, the music they prefer is a key component to their self-image and also is what links them to their peer group. Brielle described a student-centered approach to teaching that focused specifically on musical identity.

Well, at the beginning of the school year, I have the students actually do a musical profile of themselves … it's kind of like a "get to know me" but it all refers to music.

So, it talks about their preferences: what genre do you like? What is your favorite song? When you close your eyes, what do you hear? What kind of instrument do you like to play? They set a goal for themselves in music. And each nine weeks, they kind of build upon that because, hopefully, we're expanding what they like; we're broadening their horizons.

Massimo described using the circle activity referred to in the vignette found at the beginning of this chapter.

This was the very first assignment for all my classes from guitar to history of rock. The students are asked to make representations of their musical DNA by creating circle diagrams of their musical histories. The diagrams were awesome for me to go through, but the really cool thing was seeing kids pair up and asking questions like "oh, that's a really cool song—I grew up with that, how did you come across that?" and now all of the sudden, we are bonding and engaging over similar interest in music. These kids don't even know each other, and they haven't even met each other in person. It was such an easy way to create community and to allow students to embrace diversity. The next two classes we spent time just forming that common appreciation for music. It was just really cool for the kids to see that while we are different, there are some similarities.

When the outbreak of the Covid-19 pandemic in the U.S. required schools to move to remote instruction in March of 2020, many teachers found that their ability to get to know their students had been compromised in some ways and intensified in others. Jill mentioned that the remote instructional setting provided her high school faculty with a virtual "window" into aspects of their students' lives that they had not seen before.

So, it really opened our eyes to how families live because the kids you know were supposed to be on camera and they wouldn't turn on their cameras … Finally, the teacher would say, "Come on everybody turn on the camera" and "Turn on your microphone" and the chaos in the background and the eight people living in the family. The things that are hidden from us were shown to us.

On the other hand, Lena discussed her frustration with trying to negotiate the limitations of technology when it came to making connections with her students.

Not knowing enough about my kids would be one of the most challenging things, particularly this year teaching remotely. All of my music classes are still online, even though the kids are on campus and I'm on campus we meet online and so it's been very challenging for me to get to know them and to know what my students value … what they like, and I've worked [very hard] to structure opportunities for feedback in class or on their Seesaws [classroom app for communicating with students and their families], but there are still kids I'm not hearing from or students, maybe not even knowing what they like at that age and so without in-person interaction, it's really hard for me to be totally responsive to them.

Luis echoed Lena's sentiments.

I don't know what it is, but when you're in person, you can have proximity, you can talk to the kids. I can poke this kid if he's falling asleep; but if they're through a screen, I can scream, I could do this but, if they're doing that or watching the TV, there's nothing I can do. So, it's challenging in that way.

Strategies for Getting to Know Your Students

- Have students complete a personal profile inventory. Solicit information about their interests, hobbies, music preferences, goals, and aspirations.
- Ask parents to fill out a similar questionnaire at the beginning of the semester that requests information about their musical background and that asks them to identify any relatives who play or sing. Not only do you learn about your students' family life, but you also identify valuable family resources. You might find that you are able to tap into the expertise of a culture bearer and also validate your students' musical heritage.
- Get to know how your students engage with music outside of school. Make an effort to attend musical performances that are not necessarily related to school. You can learn a lot about different aspects of your students' musicianship when you have the opportunity to see them perform other genres of music. You can also use their understanding and performance of music outside of school to form bridges to understanding music learned within the music classroom.
- Get to know about how your students spend leisure time outside of the music classroom. Attending sporting events and other activities in which your students are involved can help you view your students in new ways.
- If you do not live in the same neighborhood as the students you teach, and there are faculty and staff members in the school who do, talk with them about their neighborhood experiences. You might learn more about your students' cultural lives by speaking to people who are a part of the community.
- Drive around the school and locate landmarks (the closest library, post office, grocery store). Stop and talk to people you see (people working in their yards, the postal carrier, clerks at local shops). Visit the stores closest to the school. Are there music shops in the area? What other specialty shops are available to your students?
- Create opportunities for students to talk with you about their musical and non-musical goals and aspirations.

Creating a Supportive Classroom Environment

Vignette

Ms. Johnson began teaching middle school strings at a school with a bad reputation. She described her first few days at the school as feeling like she was entering a war zone. Angry shouts could be heard in the hallway and there were frequent fights among the students. The students in Ms. Johnson's classes entered the classroom sullen and non-cooperative. Many of the students had been placed in the music classroom against their wishes by counselors looking for ways to deal with behavior problems. The students were disrespectful to Ms. Johnson and to each other.

Rather than feeling defeated, Ms. Johnson believed she could be a positive influence on the students. She chose to "enter each class with a smile" but also with a firm disposition as a no-nonsense teacher who would not tolerate misbehavior or rude comments. She treated her students with respect and demanded they do likewise. She made it a point to let her students know she believed in them, and that she would not accept anything less than their best.

Ms. Johnson felt it was important to create a supportive environment (both physically and emotionally) for all her students. She thought about the physical arrangement of the room and realized that having music folders located in a small area by the door led to students shoving and pushing to get to their seats. She made a point of walking around the classroom and sitting in seats located in different areas of the classroom to get a feeling for the space. She quickly realized how confining the set-up felt and rearranged the shelves and chairs so that students could easily access materials and could have enough space between the chairs to feel comfortable.

As she looked around her room, she was struck by the realization that the motivational posters and classroom decorations did not reflect the diversity of the student body. She searched for posters showing both men and women from differing ethnic backgrounds playing music. She specifically searched for posters that challenged stereotypical perceptions of what being a professional musician looked like. She also searched for posters reflecting a variety of genres, including the music her students talked about in class.

During the first week of school, Ms. Johnson led each of her classes in a discussion about classroom behavior. She openly discussed her expectations and she solicited input from her students. Together, they established a "no put-down" policy with zero tolerance for any disparaging comments. Additionally, Ms. Johnson worked to find ways to acknowledge the positive accomplishments of her students. She began calling parents with "good news" reports and she sent home bi-weekly email newsletters highlighting her students' success stories.

Reflective prompt: How did Ms. Johnson's actions reflect a "student-centered" approach to teaching?

In Their Own Words: Perspectives on Music Education

The vignette above illustrates how a teacher can develop a supportive environment that takes into consideration the three aspects of classroom environment: (1) relationship variables, (2) personal growth goal orientation variables, and (3) variables related to system maintenance and change (Trickett and Moos, 2002). Establishing an instructional environment that is supportive and where learners feel safe requires teachers to consider both the emotional and physical needs of the students. In the following scenario, Allen underscored the importance of validating his students' achievements as he worked to build a new paradigm for his instrumental music program.

> *We weren't developing a marching band program and I wasn't interested in competitions and my criteria for success was so far removed from what [my colleagues'] criteria for success was ... When [my students] started, it was like "Well, we're not good, we're not good." And I'd say, "I've seen you play on Sunday morning. That's not an issue. 'Good's' not an issue. It's different. But don't fool yourself into thinking that this is better or worse than" ... and they really just stopped comparing themselves. That was a big step, when they stopped comparing themselves to what other schools were doing and took pride in what they were doing.*

Allen had to make it alright to be different by focusing on the strengths of his students and developing a sense of pride in a new paradigm. Leonora likewise discussed how important it was to connect with her students and help them take pride in what they did in the classroom.

> *I composed the Tiger Pride chant just to get kids to get on the same wavelength about having a sense of pride about being a [name of school] Tiger; a sense of purpose for when you're here, what [name of school] Tigers do. We're supposed to learn, we're supposed to respect each other, we're supposed to have compassion, you know; have each other's back.*

Leonora understood the importance of developing positive relationships in the classroom and she worked hard to establish a safe place for all students. She described how a composition project had an unexpected benefit of supporting positive relationships among her fourth-grade students. As the students worked collaboratively to create an original composition, they began to value each other's input and they were proud of what they accomplished as a group.

> We started off with groups bickering, "Yeah, that's stupid" … yada-yada-yada … "Why'd you say that?" "Well, what'd you have?" "Nothing." You know, so it was all that stuff going on. And then I said, "Let me ask, is it more productive to cut each other down or try to help each other out? Because this is your song, this is going to be your song. I know you don't realize it yet, but this is going to be one of the best songs that anybody has ever composed." I already was planting seeds of success, even though at the time they would say "We ain't' writing no songs for real. We don't know how to write no songs." And so, every week we would go through one process, just getting them to respect one another's ideas … going fast forward, it went from bickering and cutting people up to "Oh, this is nice!" "Well, what do you all think about this melody?" "Oh, that's OK, alright."

Audrey also described the importance of the relationships among her students.

> [I]t is important that they are good to each other, and they care about each other. Then they feel free—like they can make mistakes and it's OK. I have section leaders for every section. Sometimes I'll record parts and then, if they are making mistakes on a certain part, I'll send them into the hallway as a section and they have a recording on their iPhone (or whatever) of what they are supposed to be learning and I'll have the section leaders help them. I tell the sections that they are like a little family, and you know, they are all different, but they are important and if one person doesn't get it you have to help each other or else you aren't doing your job and I'll be disappointed. They know I'm not going to be happy if they aren't reaching out to other kids. "We are all in this together" type of a deal. It's not just my job to teach this music; they have to own it.

Several of the teachers we interviewed described teacher–student relationships built on mutual trust and respect. Whether listening to students' favorite tunes or using student suggestions for performances, teachers frequently described how they learned from their students and how the students responded positively when their music and/or ideas were validated in the classroom. Gerald (the middle school band director) described tapping into students' musical choices to strengthen both his relationship with them and their relationships with each other.

> About twice a week we do listening time. We just listen to a piece of music. One of the days, it [the piece of music] is from me—"I think this is something that is important for you to listen to, this is an important piece because … or listen to this drum circle." Something that I have found that I think is significant. The other

listenings come from their class list. I have the student answer "Why is this important to you?" "What is important about this?" "Why is this significant to you?" "There is a reason you put this down as your favorite piece, why?" It's weird—when you try to find out what makes them tick, they really get excited. "You are interested in me. Now—what?" And they will do anything. It has really turned my classroom around. What is awesome is when you play a piece, and have a student tell why it is important to them. And then you hear a few days later [another student] say, "Hey Jennifer, I loved listening to your piece. It was awesome." And I'm like, this is why we do this.

Culturally responsive teaching requires that we build a curriculum that reflects the interests and goals of our students, and in the case of music, that means finding ways to connect to the music our students prefer and practice outside of the classroom. This can, however, be challenging for those of us who do not have experience or expertise in popular music. When asked whether the music that students listened to at home had a place in her classroom, Claire replied:

I'll be straight up with you on that one. I'm not really hip on what's going on outside Black or White in popular music. You know, I mean, the kids'll tell me something, I'll go look it up cuz I wanna understand … So I learn [from the students].

Steve shared a significant instance where what had the potential to be a negative experience for some of his students turned into a positive one because he was willing to listen to his students and consider their concerns and musical interests.

One of our bass players came to me one Friday afternoon, that was the day we had chamber ensembles, and she came right up to me about three inches from my face and said, "I hate chamber music." I said, "Okay, why do you hate chamber music?" She said, "I don't like the people I'm playing with; I don't like the music I'm playing …" Boom, boom, boom, she just came right down the list. We had about three weeks left in that quarter and I said, "Okay, you're going to finish your time with the chamber orchestra, play well, you're going to do your best, and you're going to be a leader in that Ensemble. That's my expectation of you but after this is over, I want you to find four or five of your friends, and I want you to come and see me at the beginning of next quarter, and we're going to do something different with chamber music." So she did. [We had] a bass player, a cellist, we had a bassoonist, a percussionist, and another cellist and they all came to me and they said, "What are we going to do?" I kind of took a Lucy Green approach and I said, "What do you want to play? Whatever music you want to play, the world is open to you, whatever you want to play." And they sat down and they talked. It took a couple sessions for them to come up with something, but they finally decided they wanted to do Adele's Rolling in the Deep. *"Okay," I thought, "That's OK, that'll work." They put it together, and the bassoonist decided she was going to sing, Okay, here's a 12-year-old who's going to sing Adele; it's going to be interesting! I'll try and figure out how I can help her with that.*

The short version of the story is they got started and in rehearsals (and just amazing rehearsals) they picked up things so fast and they made things work and the first time I heard [the bassoonist] sing. She opened her mouth and oh my gosh. I had no idea she had that tool. I'm sitting here with goosebumps right now. They put all this together and I'm thinking things are going well, and they're really good, so we put them on the concert. This is a formal orchestra concert and we did chamber ensembles in between. They come out to play. I get them all set up with the keyboard and other kinds of stuff and you can hear a little murmur in the crowd as I do, some things are a little different. There's a bucket drum down front, keyboard in the back, bass and cello, and a microphone and [the students] came out, they started playing and singing and they get to the first verse and everyone is cool with that, and then they opened up … spontaneous applause! People on their feet, it was a most unbelievable session to watch these five kids who never thought they were musicians to begin with, to do that, to put that together and bring their music into that room. That started the beginning—they have continued to play together, writing their own music, doing gigs—doing their own stuff. They've moved on but they still get to see each other and do some stuff. But this all started with a student coming to me and saying "I hate this," and the culturally responsive training that I'd had at that point taught me to respond in a way that allowed the students to bring themselves to the process instead of the band director part of me that would have beat them down into submission and would say, "Learn how to do this, kid," instead of saying, "You know way more than this and I'm going to empower you to use it."

Leonora often tells her students: *Never be afraid to share something with me because I learn from you, too*, and she acts on this statement. Leonora described working on the Ben E. King song, "Stand By Me" for the school's fifth-grade graduation. A group of Hispanic students approached her after class and asked if she had heard the version of the song by Prince Royce, a singer of Latin pop and rhythm and blues music styles. She admitted not knowing him but told them she would look him up on YouTube. After viewing the Spanish remix version performed by Prince Royce, Leonora rearranged the piece to include Spanish text in the students' performance.

Those students that approached me couldn't believe that I had the audacity to plug that in, but they enjoyed it. And I noticed that they sang it, they loved the Ben E. King version but being able to come in and out of [the two versions], they were on it.

Both Claire and Leonora acknowledged the gap between the music they knew and the music their students brought to the classroom. They were both able to connect to their students by learning from them. John described how he was able to connect to his students' musical background, not by using their music but by recognizing and valuing how they responded musically.

> We get a lot of students from a lot of different backgrounds. When we are teaching a song and I notice a child has found a groove to the song or something … I normally pick up on that. I try to teach the groove to everyone, or I say, "Can you do that again? I wonder if everyone can do that?" That is to encourage that student who is doing that to know that their natural response to music is valid and useful, not just to them but to everyone else.

Whether learning from their students, consciously working to stay current on musical trends, or tapping into their students' musical responses, these teachers found ways to connect their lessons to what the students brought to the classroom. They created a safe environment by valuing their students' preferences and making meaningful connections between different music genres.

Strategies for Creating an Instructional Environment that Welcomes and Values Diversity

- Critically evaluate the visual materials (i.e., posters, pictures in textbooks, videos) that students encounter in your classroom. Do they depict people of diverse backgrounds and abilities engaging with music (conducting, composing, performing, critiquing, teaching)?
- Make posters (or assign as a project to your students) that focus on musicians from your community and that reflect the cultural backgrounds of your students.
- Spend the day as one of your students. Either assign a student conductor or ask your principal to hire a substitute. Experience what it is like to walk in with the group and sit in different locations. Does everyone see and hear the same thing? Are some locations directly in the teacher's line of sight while others are hidden from view? What does it look like to be a percussion player in the back of the room compared to a saxophone player surrounded by other instruments? Can your tenor section see the conductor? Do the acoustics provide a balanced sound for the musicians? What is it like to sit on the floor in the general music classroom? What is it like to move from one location in the classroom to another?
- Video record a series of lessons from different vantage points in your classroom. As you watch the videos, critically analyze your teaching. Do you focus on certain students or certain groups of students? Do you use vernacular phrases, humor, or sarcasm in a way that could be misunderstood? What does your body language say to the students? How do your students look and sound as they enter the room? How would you describe the first five minutes of class? The last five minutes?

- Collaborate with your students in developing expectations for acceptable classroom behavior and procedures. When students have opportunities to contribute to the establishment of a safe environment, they are more invested in maintaining it.
- Think carefully about how your interactions with your students reflect your attitudes about cultural difference. Is your teaching biased in favor of mainstream ways of knowing and learning? Do you have difficulty valuing the diversity represented among your students? Do you see cultural difference as an instructional problem needing to be solved, rather than a characteristic that can be valuable in teaching and learning?

Making Program and Curricular Choices that are Culturally Responsive

Vignette

At Jackson High School, the band and choral programs offer students a variety of ways to engage with music. The band and choral directors both make curricular choices that take into consideration the demographics of their student population, what they know about how their students engage with music outside of the classroom, and how they can effectively develop their students' musicianship in relevant and meaningful ways.

Mr. Chester, the band director, believes that a successful band program is one in which his students have access to a variety of different performing ensembles. Consequently, the band program includes a jazz ensemble, a guitar class, a drumming ensemble (which performs music from cultures of West Africa, as well as cultures in South America), a steel pan ensemble, and a marching band. As a result of the variety of options in his instrumental program, a large percentage of the school's student population is involved in band. The students play frequently in the community in churches, restaurants, festivals—they are able to play in different types of community venues because of the variety of ensembles represented in the band program, ranging from more to less formal, large groups and small groups, groups that performed traditional band literature, and groups that performed popular music and music originating from specific cultures and ethnic groups. In addition, because the music that the students played from some cultures was learned aurally, they often improvised and experimented with the music that they played.

Ms. Martin's choral program is primarily comprised of what would typically be referred to as "traditional ensembles." She has a beginning mixed choir comprised of freshmen and any other students who are taking choir for the first time; a mid-level mixed choir of sophomores, juniors and seniors, and an advanced, select mixed ensemble of 16 juniors and seniors.

Ms. Martin believes strongly that her students should experience masterworks from the Western European classical tradition but she also knows that she has to provide a bridge between what they listen to at home and what she is working on in her choral program. She works hard to stay relevant by listening to the radio and familiarizing herself with popular music. By doing so, she is able to use music they know to teach different concepts. For example, she recently used a Taylor Swift song to teach the concept of duple meter and contrasted that with another pop song by Fun (the introduction to "Carry On") to teach the concept of triple meter. She also includes spirituals and representative pieces from different countries. Ms. Martin has found that her students particularly enjoy music written by some of the more contemporary composers such as Eric Whitacre or Gerald Finzi. Her students are drawn into contemporary music because it has something "fresh" to offer such as multi-meter phrasing or cluster chords.

Although Mr. Chester and Ms. Martin have slightly different approaches, they both would say their band and choral music programs at Jackson high school are successful because they each make an effort to connect with what students know and are interested in musically. They believe the success of their programs could also be measured by whether their students choose to continue to be involved with music after they graduate.

Reflective prompt: How did each of the teachers in the vignette bridge the cultural gap between home and school?

In Their Own Words: Perspectives on Music Education

Being culturally responsive means that teachers work to make informed curricular and programmatic choices that connect to what they know about their students. A variety of sources can provide information to assist teachers in making meaningful choices for their students. Zoey, an orchestra director in a middle and high school, talked about the benefit of having conversations about repertoire with her colleagues whose cultural backgrounds are different from hers.

> Both of my band colleagues are both people of color and so generally, when we have those conversations, we seem to already be on the same page … especially when it comes to repertoire choices … about choosing music that is relevant to the students. So, we haven't talked about it in great detail, but I feel like they already know … anything that I might say, they already know. I'm not here to tell anyone how to do their job, and so I get the sense that we don't really need to have much of those conversations.

For Leonora an important first step in her planning of instructional content is to look to her students as a source of information and guidance for structuring her teaching.

> *I believe that teachers learn just like students learn. I believe that students tell you what they need to know ... What I need to know from them is, what do I need to teach you based on what you're bringing in here? We could start at that point and then go from there as opposed to me thinking—you know, just setting up my whole year with lesson plans without even meeting my classes, without even seeing the personality of the class itself, and just saying, "This is what we're gonna do, because this is what I think you need to know."*

As we mentioned earlier, there is a self-perpetuating model of music education that maintains a traditional approach to secondary music education. This is reflected in the commercial world as well as in the structure of music education. For example, method books that are commonly available often connect directly to traditional Western instruments and are based on symphonic band, concert choir, and string orchestra models of instruction. Gerald recognized this and described how, as a culturally responsive teacher, he had to challenge the traditional perceptions promoted in commercially advertised instructional materials.

> *[Culturally responsive teaching] requires you to think outside the box. The easy answer lies right here in the box, but in regard to this specific goal that I have set for myself and our program and my students, it really requires you as the teacher and the students to think outside the box. Seek the answer outside where we normally would get it. The easy answer is right here. Now I have to get resources outside the book. I'm having to bring people in that I have never thought about bringing in to talk to my students before ... It is finding the resources that are not packaged up for you nicely in the textbook. It's thinking outside the box.*

As Zoey noted, providing repertoire that reflects music beyond the Western European classical tradition takes time, effort, and thought.

> *What I do is, I supplement with other things, and I skip some songs. There's a list [in a music educators' social media group] of all the different songs in those books that come out of [black face] minstrelsy and so I've been trying to kind of skip over those. There's a thing that I do where I use the students' music as audio examples rather than things like that. The question [from some of her colleagues] a lot of times is, "Well, why are you changing things? This is a book that's been used for years and years. Why do you need to do anything else?"*
>
> *Most of the time [her students] like it. I have had some pushback over* Jingle Bells *specifically. And I try not to get too much into the weeds on that one because I don't*

think getting into a political argument with kids is what I should be doing. There is a lot of pushback in my area when it comes to religious diversity, when it comes to decentering Christianity. So, I do experience some push back there, but mostly it's been pretty favorable. If we're doing a listening exercise and they hear a song that was on their music identity project, then I'll hear, "That's my favorite song!" So I love that.

Challenging the status quo was a theme that ran through many of our interviews. Claire described how she worked to get her students to challenge the dominant paradigm connected to string music education. She worked hard to disrupt any preconceived ideas her students had about what music styles and genres were available for string players and about who played traditional stringed instruments such as violin, viola, cello, and string bass.

Every year … we've brought a player of diverse background [to the school] and it doesn't always have to be classical music. I tell my kids they don't have to do classical, but they do have to have good "chops" … good technique. They can pursue jazz, they can pursue hip-hop, they can do fiddle music, they can do Celtic music, they can do anything they want to do, as long as they have everything going with their bow hold and their technique. So, anything's possible!

Claire began to question the image of school orchestras over time as she realized the disconnect between her students and the classical orchestra world. Allen knew early on in his career that he wanted to create something different. He believed that maintaining the traditional model hindered certain groups of students from participating in school music. To develop an open-door policy, he developed a unique program that had several entrance points for students interested in learning to play a musical instrument.

My music program was modular—what I was doing in my guitar class, I was hoping I could get a bunch of those students into the jazz band as well … [W]hen I was thinking about my percussion ensemble, I was thinking about, alright, what if these kids show up next year for the regular band program or for drum line—for marching band drum line, how will I make sure that they have the skills they need so that they can be part of drum line if they decide to do it? So, in all those classes, I started thinking about how it functioned as modules of the larger whole. And we talk about community too. What I really, really wanted to do is build a community of students that played music. I always joke my greatest goal in life was to be able to—when I left my job, if they don't hire another music instructor, that the music program would continue because … once you give [students] the basic skills, they're pretty amazing at continuing and doing things with it.

Challenging the status quo is a part of culturally responsive teaching, but finding the right alternatives is not easy. We have noticed that when we talk about culturally responsive pedagogy, people's first reactions tend to center around music choices. While we do see a value in expanding the types of music used for instruction, including world music or focusing on pop and hip-hop is not necessarily the answer. Lloyd discussed some important considerations when trying to provide ethnic and cultural diversity in the content of his high school choral curriculum.

> [Y]ou have to be careful. You can't assume every Black kid in choir has gospel experience in their background. They may or may not, but some of them will and so sometimes if you have kids who have a particular experience [or] expertise, someone in their family that can help out, I think it is good to bring that into the discussion. Maybe have them come and give a little more background—education about how this works, how to do it right.

Compared to some of the other teachers we interviewed, Audrey is more traditional in terms of the repertoire she selected for her choral program. She wanted her students to experience music they might not hear at home. Nevertheless, the way in which she introduced Baroque style to her advanced choir as they prepared to work on Handel's *Messiah* was a good example of using musical contexts that the students understand to form a bridge to new learning.

> If I know where they are coming from, I can make the music more exciting for them. For example, whenever I introduce Baroque music, I say, "Guys, this is our JAM. Baroque music just has a JAM to it because of the Baroque bounce, like the harpsichord is just drumming that beat and it has a good bass, the basso continuo. It's music you just want to get down to." Sometimes, when we are doing something like the Hallelujah Chorus, we'll make up beats to it.

Both Lloyd and Audrey made careful choices about the music they studied in class because they knew the music was the vehicle for developing their students' musicality. Culturally responsive teaching is a mindset that requires careful thought in regard to content, context, and instruction. In thinking about his perspectives on teaching, John came to an important realization that, for him, captured the significance and value of culturally responsive teaching as good pedagogical practice.

> You know, it's funny. The more I thought about it, the more I said, you know what John, music is multicultural. There isn't multicultural music—it's that music is multicultural. If I'm going to be a person that teaches children music so that they can be musical individuals, whatever life they choose for themselves, then it needs to be my job to teach—really—music in a global sense. That is where I am at this part of the journey around multicultural music. And I found that when I did that, I started teaching what we would consider, what is sometimes considered standard repertoire, I started teaching that differently. I started teaching it with the same techniques that

you use when you are using multicultural music. I thought, if we are going to do Vivaldi's Gloria, *how many people were actually around? And for students, that is a different culture for them also. That was really a really cool moment for me as a teacher. To say, hey wait, if I think about it as it really is, then I'm a better teacher and my students get more of the experience of learning everything.*

We know that many aspects of the learning environment can hinder or support student involvement (Lind, 1999; Walker & Hamann, 1995) but we also know that creating a supportive environment is not easy. The classroom environment is multifaceted with many factors contributing to or hindering student success. It is important that we get to know our students so that we can better act to mediate factors that interfere with students' engagement in learning.

Strategies for Acknowledging Ethnic and Cultural Diversity in Music Instruction

- Tune your car radio to a station you have never listened to and focus on the music. Listen critically for ways the music compares to things you are working on in class and use the music to reinforce these concepts with your ensembles.
- Make a point of attending community events that feature music which is outside your area of expertise and listen for the unique characteristics of the performances. Take notes about the similarities and differences between the music performed and the pieces you are working on with your ensemble.
- Capitalize on the musical expertise in your community and invite "culture bearers" into your classroom. Often you can find resources in your own school building by emailing the staff and faculty, asking for musicians in a specific genre or who perform on certain instruments. Contacting your students' family members or visiting local music stores and community centers can also lead to valuable community connections.
- Use song charts to help students connect to the literature you are working on in class. One of the high school choral directors we interviewed designed a song chart to use with repertoire in a foreign language. She provided space for students to write the original text followed by a word-for-word translation. The next section allowed space for students to paraphrase the text and provide specific details about how the text connected to their lives. The final section was designed to solicit action ideas from the students. Each student would assign a verb or descriptive word that corresponded to the lyrics and create a plan for performance that would reflect their idea.
- Incorporate aural music learning as a strategy in your music instruction. In many cultural communities, new music is always learned aurally. This mode of learning also lends itself to the development of improvisational skills.
- Be aware of how the language used in discussing music can sometimes be value laden. The terms that we use to describe/evaluate sound, such as

"ugly/beautiful," "in tune/out of tune," "or even "musical," can sometimes reflect conscious or subconscious aesthetic biases. Other terms such as "serious music" or referencing some music as "extra" or "in addition to" a "core" music curriculum can be perceived as exclusive as opposed to inclusive.

Summary

It is clear that teaching in a culturally responsive way is a complex and multifaceted endeavor. However, characterizing culturally responsive teaching as complex does not mean that it is unachievable. To the contrary, the stories, ideas, and strategies presented in this chapter confirm that as teachers desiring to be more culturally responsive in our instruction, we must:

1. be aware of how culture informs cognition and the learning process;
2. be willing to reflect on our own cultural conditioning and how it affects our beliefs, values, attitudes, and consequently our teaching;
3. get to know our students—their personal, cultural, and musical identities, and their musical preferences, and how all of these factors influence their motivation to learn;
4. create music classroom environments that not only support the bi-directional nature of learning (students learning from teachers and vice versa), but which also support multiple and equally viable perspectives with regard to music as a body of knowledge;
5. incorporate information from a variety of cultural resources and materials for use in music instruction, both in terms of connections with the societal, historical, and cultural contexts of the music studied and performed, and with the cultural backgrounds and knowledge bases of learners.

As we mentioned at the start of this chapter, our intent was to enable you to envision what culturally responsive teaching might look like in a variety of music instructional settings. In addition, we hope that we have provided the tools that will enable you to begin to think creatively about how you can use culturally responsive teaching to positively transform music learning in your own classrooms.

Discussion Questions

1. Think about a teacher or mentor who has inspired you. How did they get to know you? What traits did you value in them and why?
2. How do you think your early experiences in school impacts how you teach?
3. What barriers do teachers face when trying to get to know their students?
4. How would you describe both the physical and emotional environment of your classrooms?

5. What are some of the benefits and challenges for teachers providing instruction in an online environment?
6. How similar or different are the teachers described in the four vignettes to the teachers you have had or with whom you work?
7. Are there certain ways of being musical that you value above others? How did you develop your value system?
8. What beliefs do you have that both hinder and support your ability to learn from those around you?
9. How would you compare Mr. Chester's band program and Ms. Martin's choral program to other band and choral programs you are familiar with?
10. Would you characterize Mr. Chester's band program as successful? Why or why not? Would you consider Ms. Martin's music program to be a success? Why or why not?

References

Campbell, M. R., Thompson, L. K., & Barrett, J. R. (2021). *Constructing a personal orientation to music teaching: Growth, inquiry, and agency* (2nd ed.). Routledge.

Lind, V. R. (1999). Classroom environment and Hispanic enrollment in secondary choral music programs. *Contributions to Music Education, 26*(2), 64–77.

Trickett, E. J., & Moos, R. H. (2002). *Classroom environment scale: CES* (3rd ed.). Mind Garden Publishing.

Walker, L. M., & Hamann, D. L. (1995). Minority recruitment: The relationship between high school students' perceptions about music participation and recruitment strategies. *Bulletin of the Council for Research in Music Education, 124*, 24–38.

6

SCHOOL CULTURE

I think, for people who are looking to be culturally responsive teachers, the other uncomfortable conversation that we find ourselves in sometimes, are around educating our colleagues—and how do you do that? How much is it your job to educate your colleagues? How much of that is a part of your district culture? How much do teachers work with each other, help each other ... [These are] hard conversations.

John, elementary general music teacher

In this chapter, we examine how the culture of a school can support or impede culturally responsive pedagogy. Additionally, we discuss ideas for changing a school environment to one that reflects the principles and concepts of culturally responsive pedagogy. Activities and ideas specific to music instruction are included along with strategies for garnering administrative support. Policies and procedures that support the principles of culturally responsive pedagogy and help build a supportive infrastructure are illustrated through the inclusion of vignettes.

Culturally Responsive Schools in Action

Education (learning) does not occur in a vacuum. Just as the quality of the interaction between teachers and students in a specific classroom setting can foster or impede learning, so can the quality of the school culture. Teachers who believe in the significance and value of culturally responsive pedagogy in their own classrooms also will need to consider whether their school culture supports or obstructs those efforts.

DOI: 10.4324/9781003208136-9

The *Glossary of Education Reform* defines "school culture" as

> the beliefs, perceptions, relationships, attitudes, and written and unwritten rules that shape and influence every aspect of how a school functions, [as well as] the physical and emotional safety of students, the orderliness of classrooms and public spaces, or the degree to which a school embraces and celebrates racial, ethnic, linguistic, or cultural diversity.
>
> *(Glossary of Education Reform, 2014)*

This definition implies that school culture is influenced by the people who function within it (e.g., administrators, faculty, family, students, staff) as well as by the policies that determine how the school operates and by the community in which the school is located.

One way of gauging the cultural responsiveness within a school environment is to determine how the school views behavior; which behaviors are acceptable and which are considered deviant or different from the norm (Bacon, 2014). In many schools, "normal" behavior is defined as the extent to which students' ways of thinking and being reflect the values of the macro-culture. This definition does not offer much room for diversity or variety in how students might engage with schools.

Depending on their observed characteristics, different schools might be described as reflecting a negative, toxic culture or a positive, supportive culture. Schools in which the culture is negative or toxic:

1. Lack a clear sense of purpose. The teachers, staff, and administration aren't functioning with any clear educational goals in mind.
2. Have norms that reinforce inertia. The lack of will to change the status quo is pervasive and persistent.
3. Blame students for lack of progress.
4. Discourage collaboration. Thus, isolating teachers and preventing them from sharing effective instructional practices or working together to address and resolve problems.
5. Often have actively hostile relations among staff, which in turn affect students (Peterson, 2003, p. 11).

On the other hand, a positive school culture is possible when conditions necessary for maximum learning have been identified and prioritized. We know that teachers who use a culturally responsive approach to teaching in a specific instructional setting can be extremely effective with students. Likewise, if the school atmosphere is positive and supportive of students, then all stakeholders benefit.

A common thread among the educators we interviewed whose instructional and administrative approaches reflected cultural responsiveness was a recognition that what happens in classrooms must be part of a larger school culture that views cultural diversity as an asset, and which supports students both individually and collectively. They were addressing the development of a positive culture in the schools in which they teach, hope to teach, or provide administrative leadership by: (1) recognizing that re-envisioning school culture requires the investment of all stakeholders; (2) engendering student and community pride in schools that reflect cultural diversity, viewing them as assets rather than liabilities; and (3) fostering positive connections and interactions among all stakeholders.

Re-envisioning School Culture

Vignette

At the conclusion of the previous academic year, the faculty in the elementary school where Mr. Davis taught general music learned that their principal was retiring. This news came as no surprise to many of the teachers because the school had been struggling with issues ranging from students' low academic achievement and motivation to poor teacher morale. Although some faculty, including Mr. Davis, hoped that a new principal might be able to turn things around, most did not have high expectations.

At the start of the new school year, when Mr. Davis reported to the school for the first time, he could sense a difference immediately. The school interior had been freshly painted, colorful cushions had been added to the benches in the lobby, as well as a banner that read "Welcome to Spring Hill Elementary School—Our Future Begins Now!" Many faculty members were still reluctant to place much confidence in the new principal's capacity to foster change in the school. To their thinking, the challenges they faced were not going to be changed by a new coat of paint and platitudes. Mr. Davis, on the other hand, was energized by the new atmosphere.

During the first faculty meeting, the principal shared his vision for a new Spring Hill Elementary School. He welcomed feedback from all teachers regarding ways in which they could work individually and in concert to support students, and to support and encourage each other, so that they could develop a sense of community. Mr. Davis began to think about how he could help foster a positive school climate. He came up with the idea of having a moment once a month when everyone in the school would come together in a themed assembly. Children and teachers would sing songs, read stories and poems, recognize birthdays, and celebrate staff members' and students' achievements. The assembly would end with everyone singing the school song. Mr. Davis thought the assemblies could be held at the beginning of the month to get everyone off to a good start, or they could be held during the final week of the month to end the month in a positive way. He shared the idea with two other classroom teachers, the art teacher and the PE teacher, and together they met with the principal to share their ideas. The principal decided to try it out for three months.

Reflective prompt: What factors might encourage or inhibit efforts to change a school climate from negative to positive?

In Their Own Words: Perspectives on Music Education

I find my school is one of those places where we talk about our diversity a lot, we talk about the diverse students, but I'm not sure we have a concerted effort to teach as a diverse school. To teach—that global citizenship piece … We talk more about diversity than we do about diversity.

John's description suggests that his elementary school has not yet managed to move beyond merely giving lip service to cultural diversity to actually engaging in practices that would create a positive school environment for all students. In this regard, his school is not unlike many schools across the nation. How do schools begin the process of acknowledging and embracing the cultural diversity of their student populations?

One way to begin is for teachers, administrators, and staff to combine efforts to create a positive school culture. When a positive climate is established school-wide, it can be even more supportive to students and expand upon what individual teachers achieve with culturally responsive pedagogy within the classroom. This is where administrators like Jill play a significant role in establishing a supportive school culture by being intentional about the faculty and staff they select for their schools.

You know, as a hirer of teachers, I wonder how this is being approached in college training, university training or pre-service training. Because what I've seen (and you know, teachers are candid about this), it takes a while in a building before you come around. When I came to this school, it was not very culturally responsive, and it's taken a big turnover in staff from top to bottom for us to meld and be all rowing in the same direction. And so, I would like to see it addressed or I wonder how can it be addressed authentically? Because you can say to somebody, "Well, I'm going to do a simulation and imagine you had 12 kids and four are Black and four are White and four are Brown." Man, it's just assumptions like crazy. It's just assumptions. And so, there's always a danger in that.

Luis also believes that the attitudes of faculty in a school can go a long way toward promoting a learning environment that is supportive and culturally responsive to students' needs.

> *I feel like the nature of our school, because we call ourselves an international school and we are promoting diversity, it has attracted teachers that are already on board to that idea. And then, because, thankfully, our school has been doing this kind of weekly [professional development] about studying this book [Culturally Responsive Teaching and the Brain by Zaretta Hammond, 2015] and having a lot of really intimate conversations I would hope, so I think we're all on the same page in terms of wanting to be as culturally responsive as we can.*

But creating a positive, supportive school culture goes beyond the kind of personnel that comprise a school. According to Jill, effective re-visioning of school culture means that the new vision should permeate all aspects impacting how the school functions.

> *I always say the vision of the school is in the master schedule and the vision of the schools is in the budget and so as a matter of serving kids, I mean, it's just kind of a Maslow's [hierarchy of needs] type thing. Yeah, sometimes the teaching and certainly the test scores are the last thing we're worrying about because we want the kid to feel safe and not worried about being deported. Or you know, escaping whatever happened in the neighborhood on the weekend. And so, the conversations very often are about (as principals particularly), we have site-based budgeting. Like I have $14 million that I program for my school for next school year to hire, to train, to provide for all the kinds of kids in my school and we have all kinds. So, it comes most often in strategic planning, I think. Not so much about classroom instruction, but rather, what kind of shifts in programming are we making?*

Gerald, the middle school band director, talked about the transformation in culture that occurred in his school over the last several years.

> *The school atmosphere has changed a lot, even since I've gotten here. This is my 4th year, we have a new administrator, and we had a different administrative team the previous three years. The atmosphere this year is positive. Students and faculty. We kind of now have a feeling of community and a unified goal. Everyone loves to be a [named the school mascot]. The community involvement has increased significantly. Now we understand that we are just part of the big picture, we are part of student success, we are one aspect of that, all parts of the machine have to be well oiled to work. It is constantly like, do you need help with something, what can I do? Can I help you with something? I need help in my classroom. Community, please come in and provide us with support. Now it is like we are working hand in hand on the success of the kids.*

Leonora described a similar atmosphere of unified effort in her elementary school, though it did not happen overnight.

> *The [school] atmosphere this year is great. The children, they smile, [and] even if they are not smiling, and you insist, if you say, "Good morning!" [they respond] "Good morning." "Yeah, it is a good morning, isn't it?" "OK." You know, you have those interactions that let the kids know that they are in a safe place; it's like they know that. Well, with this being the third year that this administration has been here, I think the staff is a little more trusting. Cuz, you know, whenever you make an administrative transition, there's mistrust, you know. The administrator comes in like "I don't care what you did before, this is the way it is." And then it comes to, "you know, some of the things y'all did before weren't so bad." So, I think relationships between administration and staff are better. The relationships amongst colleagues have, for the most part, always been pretty good, you know. Very cordial.*

Teachers and parents partnering for the benefit of better learning outcomes for students was a significant focus of effort in Claire's elementary arts magnet school.

> *We're very much aware of our demographics and testing and … how to partner better with families. I know at our school, we have workshops to help parents learn how to teach their child how to read and phonics and like whatever we're doing, especially with reading and writing, we have workshops where parents are invited to come and participate … So building community's huge—and trust.*

Pre-service teachers like Stew are also thinking about how they can create positive and supportive spaces within and beyond their classrooms.

> *It's one thing to talk about these practices in [methods] class but to actually implement it in a meaningful way is something totally separate. It's going to vary with every class that comes into your classroom. It's very adaptable or you have to be adaptive in that way. I've been writing down important information and ideas I've talked about with mentors and colleagues, and I'm hoping I've done enough preparation that I can implement some of these practices in a meaningful way for my students.*

Each person's descriptions indicate how they or their respective schools or districts provided support for a positive school culture, which is a foundational necessity if culturally responsive pedagogy is to be effective. Music educators will want to find ways in which they can initiate and or contribute to school-wide efforts to promote a school climate that is inclusive and positive for teachers, students, parents and the community at large.

An initial step toward re-envisioning the culture of a school from negative to positive involves the staff and administrators identifying and assessing the values and norms of the school that characterize the school culture. The next step involves deciding which of these aspects of school culture are positive and should be maintained and strengthened, and which are negative and need to be changed. Professional staff development is one way in which faculty and administrators can begin to craft ways to effect meaningful change in school culture. The need for specific types of professional development can arise from a variety of events—some curricular and others societal. Many of those we interviewed indicated that the protests surrounding the murder of George Floyd in May 2020 was a catalyst for subsequent professional staff development. For example, Luis observed:

> the week after [the death of George Floyd], our principal said we're going to be doing … some DI [diversity and inclusion] work when we read Zaretta Hammond's book, Culturally Responsive Teaching and the Brain, so we had assignments every week and we've been doing that all year. But I really can't recall doing anything before that, in terms of explicitly culturally responsive teaching.

Lena emphasized the influence of the principal's role as educational leader in engaging faculty and staff with professional development that can result in positive changes in school culture.

> I think [one of her principals] is really well aligned with our district's statements and expectations for culturally responsive teaching … So primarily, like student-centered learning with Black and Brown kids in mind. And he's getting training in anti-racist education, making sure the staff is getting training, so I think he has a competent understanding and a growing practice. But his mindset is also really flexible, so when those of us with more experience or more training say, "hey, we need to adjust," then he's like, "of course," you know, "what can I do to help?"

Likewise, Luis also described the benefits of having an administrator who had a vision for the school in terms of teaching students through a culturally responsive lens and sought to provide opportunities for professional staff development to realize that vision.

> I think that my principal—she's great—she's White and I think she, on some level, is trying to find as many resources as she can, and I think right now it's hard, because everyone is trying to book everybody to come and do talks, which is on one hand great. On the other hand, everyone's doing it right now and it's not possible. So I think she's trying her best. She's doing what she can, but she understands that this is what is needed, especially at our school, but at every school, so I feel really supported in that way. I feel really, really supported in the way that she understands that this is vital for not only our school's growth, but our kids' growth and their brains and if we pride ourselves in talking about raising a whole child, from all aspects emotionally and everything, then this is a huge part of it.

Especially if they're growing up in New York, where you walk outside and everyone in the world is right there; everyone's different and you're on the subway and it's part of your life. I think it's really important and I'm thankful that she sees that. It just has to manifest itself into our everyday PD [professional development], every meeting, everything.

Garnering administrative support for creating a school culture that supports diverse students isn't always easy, even when the changes suggested are doable, but could have a significant impact on how included students may feel. Zoey describes her experiences in trying to engender small changes in her school.

There are some things that I've only occasionally talked to my administrators about culturally responsive teaching and in one case it was when we had scheduled field day during Ramadan, and I had wanted to suggest that we maybe move it to a more inclusive time. And I generally got the idea that I was suggesting something that nobody thought was important … I also had a conversation one time about maybe, including other holidays in our December celebrations, rather than just everything being about Christmas, and I was basically told that everybody else was less important. That was the gist of what the person said to me.

Allen's high school experienced a sudden, substantial, and unanticipated increase in students whose primary language was not English. Most of the students were from Mexico. As Allen explained, the school district's response to this new situation provided teachers in the high school with the support they needed to meet the instructional needs of the new students.

[T]he district has done a pretty good job of constant staff development on how to work with [the Mexican students]—it's interesting now because now it's a population of teachers that have functioned in that environment for a length of time, but in those beginning years, there was a lot of resistance; there was [also] a lot of staff development to make sure that those instructors were following best practices and, even to the extent that they would get grants to send teachers to Vera Cruz, Mexico so that they had a better understanding of the educational practices that were happening where the students were coming from too. And that was effective because people would come back and say, "I had no idea—I had no understanding of why my student was acting like this—now I understand."

Although staff development of this type is valuable at the school level, similar types of staff development at the district level can focus attention on the need to collaborate across schools to achieve positive school climates—particularly in the relationship between feeder schools. Lloyd, a high school choral director, described how his school district is making efforts to dialogue about issues of race as a factor influencing and impacting learning.

We have a whole … they call them courageous conversations. We have a whole framework for how to approach those conversations. Are you coming from a feeling point of view, from a cognitive thinking point of view; are you coming from a personal point of view? And then we have certain things we are supposed to keep in mind. For example, this is a difficult conversation for everyone to have. It is going to feel uncomfortable. Let's recognize that. It may not resolve anything; it may not end in a resolution. That's OK, everyone has to speak their own truth. What your experience has been is true for you [regardless of] whether others agree or have had the same experience. Part of it is setting up a framework for having conversations both as a faculty and with students and with community members on issues where race is maybe particularly sensitive.

The idea of fostering positive school culture between and among several schools could be particularly significant in the context of music education. It is not uncommon for music teachers who serve "feeder" schools to collaborate on their programs to provide consistent instruction.

Gerald described how he came to an illuminating realization in this regard that helped him more clearly understand how important culturally responsive teaching could be for his specific instructional situation.

Every year, I do a retention report of eighth graders going on to high school because I remember being a high school director how important that was and that tends to be a time when we will lose students, going from middle school to high school … I decided to look at the three individual programs that we feed into to look specifically at how many students do I have going to this high school are actually going, and the other [high schools] as well. The three different high schools have three unique marching styles. One is what I would refer to as a corps style … the other one I've defined as "outdoor pageantry" … and then the last one is show style marching band. When I looked at my retention to the corps style, it was at 100% every year. Going to the "outdoor pageantry" school, we were at 90% or above. What was alarming was when I took a look the students who were supposed to be going to the "show style" band. And in my three years of being there [at the school] I had no students continue on in high school band there. That was disturbing and alarming to me … what am I doing that students aren't wanting to continue on with that band program? It's a strong band program; just different. And when I reflected on the year and looked back at my previous lesson plans, I realized every time we spoke or talked about marching band, it was always in relation to the other two styles. I never showed any videos or provided any examples of "show style." And kind of nonchalantly, I was pushing that to the side, making … almost providing that it wasn't important. So that's what kind of drove me … I've got to change the way I'm teaching and the influence I have on these students that all three styles are important, all three styles are good; they're just different.

As Gerald began to understand the nature and value of culturally responsive teaching, he also was able to recognize that he and his colleagues often were using facets of culturally responsive teaching without realizing it.

> We did a professional development with the band directors this fall which had to do with vertical alignment. So students who come from this group of elementary schools that feed into this group of middle school who go to this high school. Making sure we are all on the same page. What I found interesting with these conversations that I was a part of, a big chunk of it was culturally responsive teaching. Being aware of where students are from, their experiences, what's important to them, are we including that in our instruction ... Although the purpose had to do directly with curriculum from the state for the workshop, I found us spending a lot of time talking about culturally responsive teaching. So was it set up to be like that? No, but it turned into that.

Gerald's observation emphasizes that a disposition toward culturally responsive teaching corresponds with factors associated with effective teaching in general. The interesting aspect of Gerald's account is the implication that, to some extent, teachers were already engaging in behaviors that could be construed as culturally responsive, though they may not have been aware of it. Certainly, one reason that Gerald was able to recognize that the conversations generated during the band directors' professional development session included a culturally responsive facet was because he was familiar with the principles of culturally responsive pedagogy.

Engendering Pride in Schools that are Culturally Diverse

Vignette

At the beginning of Ms. McDonald's first year teaching chorus at a high school with a student population that was predominantly African American, she began as she always did: by teaching the Alma Mater to each choir in the school. In the case of this particular school, the melody of the Alma Mater was based on the Canadian National Anthem. Ms. McDonald found a hymn-like arrangement of the Anthem and adapted it for use with the choirs.

When she began teaching the arrangement to her advanced choir, the students asked if she could "jazz up" the arrangement in a way similar to what they had seen in a recent movie where a school song had been rearranged in a style that students felt was more relevant. Ms. McDonald was not certain that she could do it, but told the students that if they would learn the hymn arrangement of the Alma Mater, she would work on creating an alternate, "jazzier" arrangement.

By the time the students had learned the "traditional" version of the Alma Mater, Ms. McDonald had created an alternate arrangement and decided to try it with her advanced choir first, since the group was comprised of juniors and seniors. Ms. McDonald knew that if the new arrangement met with their approval, the other choirs would accept it enthusiastically. As the choir began learning the new arrangement, they were increasingly excited by the style of it, and to Ms. McDonald's surprise, some of the students began to improvise vocally during certain sections of the song in ways that enhanced the performance. The students liked the new arrangement so much that they begged to be able to premiere their version at the next school-wide assembly. Ms. McDonald agreed. At the next assembly, the reception of the song by faculty, students, and administration was so positive that it became the preferred version performed by the choirs for special events at the school.

Reflective prompt: What message do you take from the vignette regarding ways to honor students' ideas and connect with them in meaningful ways? How do we listen to the voices calling for change and still honor the traditions of the past? Is this balance necessary?

In Their Own Words: Perspectives on Music Education

As we have seen thus far, many factors come together to contribute to a positive school culture. Among them, the most crucial is determining what values and standards represent an environment where difference is not only accepted but also valued. This means being intentional about developing a culture of belonging and community within the school.

Debra's description of her high school choral students' reactions when they attended music festivals at another high school suggested that the students already identified and internalized values that they believed represented who they were as a school community.

> We are an IB (International Baccalaureate) school; we do IB classes, but we aren't [names another school]. I think there is a real sense of pride, and the kids are really proud of how diverse we are. When they go to schools like [names same school] for all-county or all-state for the choir, they are really shocked at how White everyone is. Even though I only took one Hispanic and five White kids to area All State, they were all just like saying, "where are all the Black kids?" They don't feel like it is right for them, they are so used to diversity, and that makes me happy and so proud.

Pride in diversity can also take the form of students' deep satisfaction in their own musical achievements in programs that do not necessarily follow traditional models. Allen's high school band program was distinctly different from those of his colleagues. Although this difference was a result of intentional planning by Allen to meet the specific musical needs of his students, getting them to appreciate how their program differed from other high school band programs instead of viewing their program from a deficit perspective took time.

> *A big step, was when they [the students] stopped comparing themselves to what other schools were doing and, took pride in what they were doing and being out in the community too. When parents started saying, "I really appreciate this and what's happening is exciting for me," it became a lot more exciting for the school too. So once community started taking ownership of [the music program], then it became … that spiral upward where if the community took ownership of it, the kids took ownership of it.*

Sometimes, the history of a school can serve to engender pride in the students, especially if the history is illustrative of values critical to historically marginalized groups. Claire saw an opportunity to show her students how their involvement in the string program actually connected them to an important part of their school's history and, in so doing, fostered in them a sense of pride both in their string program and in their school.

> *When I first came to the school, I discovered that the namesake of the school … was president of [a local historically Black college] at the turn of the century, and I started to do research on him and I learned that he played the violin … I found a photograph of a 1912 music class when the [college] was coed, and in this photograph were two young Black men holding violins—African American men [and] women … having formal instruction and playing violin. That was a really good connection. And then I went to the [city's] historical museum … and learned as much as I could about this man. And when I shared that with my students, often times they'd say "Wow, we're part of history!" And they quickly caught on to the idea that this violin dream that [the school's namesake] had because he actually played, he actually had photographs of this violin in his papers, that's how much it meant to him. So the children immediately identified with that—that they were carrying out a legacy that started over a hundred years ago.*

Frequently, engendering pride among the members of a specific organization involves finding areas of commonality or focusing on what makes groups of people more alike than different. Sometimes, however, this can come at the expense and exclusion of those who value individuality. In the case of schools, creating a sense of community while also celebrating and valuing diversity is a delicate balance, but it is attainable when everyone involved is committed to supporting those values.

Fostering Positive Connections

Vignette

Ms. Randolph had taken over a middle school band position that formerly had been held by a good friend who was moving to another school in the district. One of the first things Ms. Randolph wanted to do was to get to know the students in her band. On their first day of rehearsal, Ms. Randolph asked them how they spent time with music outside of school. Based on their responses, Ms. Randolph made a list of activities in which her students were involved, which included playing for religious services, local festivals, and other special events in the community. Ms. Randolph resolved to attend at least one event every couple of weeks to show her students that she supported their extra-curricular musical endeavors.

One Saturday, Ms. Randolph was attending an event featuring a Javanese gamelan ensemble that included one of her band students playing the *slenthem* (a metal-barred instrument). Ms. Randolph recognized several of the Javanese young people in the group as being students at her school. She particularly noticed another young man playing a *gendèr* (another metal-barred instrument) and was impressed by his technique and musicianship. Ms. Randolph immediately went up to the second player and complimented him on his performance. She asked if he had an interest in being in the band. He told her that he used to be very interested in band, and wanted to learn to play the vibraphone, but that he soon realized he was not good enough for the band and so he lost interest. Ms. Randolph tried to press him for details, but he was reluctant to say anything more.

When Ms. Randolph got home that evening, she called the colleague who had previously held the band position at her school and asked him if he knew of the young man. Her colleague said he remembered that another teacher had approached him about placing the young man in the band. "Unfortunately," her colleague said, "he didn't read music, so I couldn't use him. To tell you the truth, that's why I decided to leave. I had a really hard time recruiting for the band. Most of the students just weren't interested in music."

"But I see them playing music everywhere in the community!" Ms. Randolph countered. The colleague sighed and said, "Yeah, well, they're just not interested in 'serious' music." At that moment, Ms. Randolph decided that she would do whatever she could to bring the young *gendèr* player into the band. To help him learn notation, she would pair him up with his peer in the gamelan ensemble who was in band. She resolved to program a gamelan piece transcribed for the percussion section of the band, which would give both young men an opportunity to display their stylistic prowess. Ms. Randolph also decided to invite the gamelan ensemble to be featured on the band concert, so that her students could experience the music in its natural form and which would almost guarantee increased attendance due to the group's popularity in the community.

Reflective prompt: Consider the ways in which, as music educators, we may overlook or reject opportunities to make critical connections with students simply because the type of musicianship they value isn't reflected in the offerings of the school music program.

In Their Own Words: Perspectives on Music Education

Teachers often must work collectively and collaboratively to promote a school environment that embraces diversity and supports all students. Sometimes that might mean having some initially uncomfortable conversations with colleagues to get a better sense of how we, as individual teachers, think about, feel about, and react to cultural diversity as well as how race, ethnicity, and culture influence students' experiences with school. John explained that for him, just thinking of starting that kind of conversation was daunting.

> *I took a class … on culturally affirming music education. [One of the participants said] "As a White guy, I feel really awkward asking a Black person his opinion on something because I'm not sure what I'm going to get. He might think, why are you asking just me? I don't want to go through that." The solution that the class came to was, well you know, you might just have to go through that a couple of times. If it is worth it for you to get the information so that you can connect with your students and give them a better educational experience, then you will go through that conversation if you have to.*

Steve also mentioned how intimidated many teachers are when it comes to both talking about cultural diversity and trying to teach in a culturally responsive way.

> *The biggest concern is … what I'm hearing from people right now is that everybody's afraid of making mistakes. I'm afraid I'm going to step on toes— I'm afraid I'm going to mention something wrong. My first response to that is, how many times are you perfect in everything else you do? You're going to make mistakes and it's okay. It's not okay if you do it out of ignorance and aren't willing to learn. We've got to be able to look at this and say, how can we go about*

making this work and making it our best honest effort in what we do? And should we make mistakes along the way, we're honest about that and we learned about that, and we grow from them. I have yet to have anyone (and I've made my fair share of all of those mistakes) and I've never had anyone come to me to point out that mistake and try to hang me for that. It's always been "I have a concern," and when I'm open to that, then I learned in that process and it's a very positive outcome.

For newer, younger music teachers, the difficulty in having "hard conversations" with colleagues sometimes stems from a perceived power differential between themselves and veteran music educators or administrators. When asked about whether she thought her colleagues and administrators knew about culturally responsive teaching, and whether she had conversations with them about it, Zoey explained:

I think some of them know, but I try not to bring it up, especially because I'm younger. I don't necessarily ever want to be seen as telling other teachers how to do their jobs. The only time I really do bring it up is I'm chair of the orchestra department here in the county, and so during department meetings, I make a point of talking about it and just making sure that the people who are working with me know that it's important to be teaching in a culturally relevant way, because one of the things that I learned is that not everybody is learning about that in their music education programs in college.

Claire acknowledged that talking with a colleague whose cultural background was different from hers helped her to better understand how culture could impact her own teaching as well as her students' learning.

I started talking to my friend, who's African American, who was teaming with me and I said, "Help me get this. I just don't get it. Help me get it." I get some of it, and I think that's another thing you can do is get to know your colleagues that are different from you. Spend some time listening to them ... You'll learn things that you were just oblivious to.

Claire's intent in connecting with her colleague was to gain a better understanding about facets of cultural diversity that only this particular colleague could provide, as a means to improve Claire's own sensitivity to how cultural differences inform and shape perspectives. Claire was fortunate in that she worked in a school where the teaching staff was culturally diverse. Perhaps most importantly, the quality of the relationships that she forged allowed her to have such conversations with colleagues whose racial, ethnic, and cultural backgrounds differed from hers.

Leonora noted that there were a few teachers in her school who consistently had problems relating to their students. She believed that teachers who face challenges with students due to cultural differences might break through that barrier if they have an opportunity to see their students in a different context. By "drawing teachers in" and trying to engage with them in positive ways, she hoped to help them develop a multidimensional view of their students that might provide them with insights into how to motivate and interest the students.

> *When certain teachers come [to music class], some of them drop [students] off at the corner [of the hallway]. And I'll say, "Hey! Good morning!" [smiling and waving]. "Good afternoon!" Then I have some that want to come [and they ask], "How did they do?" I love those, because they cared about what was going on even though they weren't here. I would like to make better connections with the ones that think, "This is my planning time, I don't care what you do with 'em," you know. To help them understand that what I do, it's not just that what I do matters, but what your children are doing is great and sometimes when they—the children really, really, have picked up on something very quickly, I'll say, "Do y'all wanna perform for your teacher?" and "Yay!!" [Then she pantomimes talking on the music classroom phone to a teacher] "Hey, they are rocking out hard today, can you come a little early?" [to see what they're doing] And the teachers will come and … sometimes I'll even notice my colleagues, sometimes they come and they look like they've had a rough day and they hear their students singing and doing whatever we've done, and they're just like, "Oh my God, this is just so wonderful!" So, you know, I try my best to just kind of reel them in, even the ones that sometimes … stand off.*

Leonora saw her music classroom as a place where students have the opportunity to demonstrate knowledge and skills that are different from what they may be asked to demonstrate in other classes. Her intent in inviting teachers to view students' musical activities was to give teachers the chance to see their students as multifaceted, multidimensional individuals.

Positive climates exist in schools where teachers, administrators, and family members recognize that their coordinated efforts can help students successfully achieve their academic goals. As Jill observed:

> *it's the element of creativity that I think can be the seat of the self. You know; that from which you generate. Whether it's music or art or performance, it is the art. It is the act of creating that I think comes most authentically to who you are at your core. Accepting that, acknowledging that, honoring that, calling that out through the arts is the most authentic, and I would say, encouraging, thing that a teacher can do to help kids put down their guard.*

Music teachers are often in a particularly good position to develop long-term relationships with families because students often participate several years in a school music program taught by the same music instructor. Claire had an eye-opening conversation with a parent about how her string program might be viewed by some segments of the community.

> *I was talking to a parent whose child was not in the string program, and she said, "well you understand not everybody wants their child playing violin if you understand the history of that—because of the connotation of the Black slave playing for the White master"—and I didn't know what she was really talking about—I mean I had to go back and sit down and do a little research. It was like—ah—I didn't know—I'd never thought about it before. She knew all about it, but I didn't know about it. You know, these were things that she was aware of that were part of her history and I was oblivious to it. And I don't want to be oblivious.*

Claire discovered that understanding the perspectives of parents, guardians, and other family members regarding the school curriculum and approaches to teaching can provide valuable insights that could help her make instruction more meaningful and effective for her students.

The following statement by Lena meaningfully encapsulates this notion of how critical collaboration is to the entire process of fostering positive connections.

> *I think I would just want to emphasize how collaborative the whole process needs to be, and teaching is collaborative anyway, but when I talk about culturally responsive teaching, I visualize this web of people all hooked together with students giving and receiving and colleagues giving and receiving and our families, giving and receiving and so I just feel really thankful for my own teachers, my own students, and the ways that all of those people are determined to move forward in love, even when it's really hard or confusing. And you know love doesn't mean no accountability—it's like with my mentor—love is tough love. But yeah, that's the thing I have started to think about this year. It's like, I'm coming off of my high horse from grad school and now I'm back in the field, and this is hard, and I just feel really grateful for that community and reciprocity of everybody who's trying to do better.*

Strategies to Foster Positive Change in School Culture

• Walk around your school and take pictures of different items: posted signs, locker decorations, bulletin boards, the entrance to the school, the hallway near your classroom. Do the items send a message of inclusion? Share your pictures with students and colleagues and brainstorm ways to create positive messaging.

• If your school is involved in a process of re-envisioning its culture, get together with other arts educators in your building and think of ways in which you can collaborate to support the goals of the school. Because teachers in the arts are more often thought of as "artists," making visible and perceptible efforts to achieve school goals will help others view you as an educator.

- Find opportunities to showcase cultural diversity in the repertoire and guest ensembles chosen for performance within the school.
- Offer to support and assist student musical groups in school that are not a part of the music program. This will broaden your musical horizons.
- Look for opportunities to expand the curricular offerings in your program so that they reflect more diverse musical expressions.
- Think carefully about how your music program will meet the unique needs of your students and develop your program accordingly. Do not be afraid to go outside the traditional models of music instruction.

Summary

In this chapter, we have proposed that culturally responsive pedagogy is most effective when it is part of a concerted school-wide effort to maximize students' academic, emotional, and social potential. One way to evaluate a school's capacity to support the kind of instruction exemplified through culturally responsive teaching is to look at the indicators of school culture and determine whether they combine to create a positive or negative climate.

The definition presented at the beginning of this chapter makes clear that a variety of factors contribute to school culture. These factors are associated with the physical space of school; the relationships, attitudes, beliefs, and perceptions of everyone who works and interacts within the school; and explicit and implicit rules and policies that govern how the school functions. Teachers who employ culturally responsive pedagogy in their classrooms understand that if they work in isolation from their school colleagues, administrators, and families, their effectiveness will be limited. Conversely, creating a school culture that is positive and supportive to students (and to everyone else engaged in the educational enterprise) enhances the aims of culturally responsive pedagogy.

Discussion Questions

1. Think about the schools you attended or in which you currently teach. How would you describe the school culture? What indicators contribute to your impression?
2. High school stereotypes such as the jock, the nerd, the cheerleader, the preppie, and the rebel are a staple of popular media. Why do you think these stereotypes persist? What do these labels imply about how teenagers view individuality and difference?
3. Do teachers and administrators have different responsibilities in promoting positive change in school culture?

4.   What opportunities might there be to take students' ideas and incorporate them in your teaching to promote the kind of *esprit de corps* that instills a sense of community within a school?

5.   What might be some of the challenges of initiating "courageous conversations" about race, ethnicity, or other issues of difference in a school? What might be some of the benefits? How different might these conservations be in a school where the faculty is racially/ethnically homogeneous as opposed to one where the faculty is more culturally diverse?

References

Bacon, M. (2014). Shaping culturally responsive school environments. *Leadership*, *43*(5), 22–25.

The Glossary of Education Reform. (2014). School culture. In *The glossary of education reform*. http://edglossary.org/school-culture/

Hammond, Z. (2015). *Culturally responsive teaching and the brain*. Generic.

Peterson, K. D. (2003). Positive or negative? *Journal of Staff Development*, *23*(3), 10–15.

7

COMMUNITY

It was interesting to watch who's taking ownership and pride ... Once the community started taking ownership of it, then it became that circle, that spiral upward where if the community took ownership of it, the kids took ownership of it. If the kids took ownership of it, the community took ownership of it.

Allen, high school band director

This chapter focuses on the school and community connection. We discuss characteristics of positive school and community partnerships in relationship to culturally responsive teaching. Ideas for including community resources into the music classroom are explored along with activities and approaches that will carry the concepts of culturally responsive teaching into a larger context.

Connecting to the Community

We have begun to acknowledge that the community plays an important role in education. We frequently hear about community engagement in education initiatives, community and service-learning projects, and partnerships that involve community organizations. Additionally, we know that our students live and learn in their communities and that the environment helps shape who they are. Throughout this book, we have stressed the importance of getting to know our students and we have discussed the importance of bridging the gap between "academic abstractions and lived sociocultural realities" (Gay, 2018, p. 37). We believe we can begin to bridge this gap by breaking down the barriers of the classroom walls and by recognizing what the community has to offer.

DOI: 10.4324/9781003208136-10

School music programs have a long and rich history of community involvement, and we often have strong ties to the community. Music groups perform at civic functions and many choral and instrumental ensembles participate in service-learning projects. Many teachers engage in community projects or service learning, not only to support music learning but also to develop citizenship skills and "produce students who are more tightly engaged in the larger communities surrounding their institutions" (Garoutte & McCarthy-Gilmore, 2014, p. 1). These activities have been important to our students, and they have provided teachers with opportunities to get to know their students outside of the classroom, but they do not always have the intended result.

There is a danger that some projects may actually be reinforcing the ideas of privilege and inequality in our students. Eby (1998) argued that the perception of privilege and power can be reinforced when community partners are treated as "subjects" rather than participants in the learning process. When students perceive they are "doing" a service rather than learning alongside their community partners, they often see themselves as being at the top of the social hierarchy. In contrast, programs that are built upon the fundamental belief that communities are "asset rich" and that learning is reciprocal, can reinforce the concepts of equality by allowing students to see and value those around them (Garoutte & McCarthy-Gilmore, 2014).

Likewise, there is a danger that the community program may be reinforcing the ideas of privilege and inequality. Steve described working in a university program originally designed to help pre-service music teachers learn to work successfully in underserved school districts. He described how the program changed over the years to one that was intended to work in tandem with public school music programs to one that worked to supplant music education in the schools.

> *It was just going to be its own little microcosm of 200 kids who are lucky enough to get into the program ... I was told by our funder there was "right" music and there was "wrong music." That was the beginning of the end for me.*

A program that was once based on equity and diversity had morphed into one that promoted a single "ideal" that traditional, Western European orchestral music was somehow better than any other type of music and that the program was doing a service to diverse students by allowing them into the classical music world.

Designing community partnerships where students are "co-creators" and "co-learners" with the community ensures a relationship where common goals can be reached. Before any bridge can be built or any meaningful project developed, educators must first learn about the community in which they teach and learn about the people who live in that community. This knowledge allows teachers to draw upon the resources and expertise that are already a part of the students' environment. By bringing the community into the classroom or by taking students outside of the school building, we hope to make meaningful connections to our students' lives and that learning will become more relevant for our students, but this does not happen without careful planning. Community projects that focus on genuine, authentic, shared experiences facilitate learning. Designing projects that draw upon the expertise of our community members, and learning about the communities that impact our students' lives, can help us build a strong foundation for culturally responsive teaching.

Getting to Know the Community

Vignette

Ms. Davison was hired to teach instrumental music at a school located 45 minutes from her home in the suburbs. The school was situated in an urban setting quite different from where she had grown up and it served a very diverse population. As Ms. Davison drove to her new classroom for the first time, she noticed there were signs in the community written in languages she did not recognize and stores in the downtown area that were not familiar to her. She stopped for a cup of coffee and the music playing in the restaurant was different than the jazz tunes that played in her neighborhood coffee shop. Although the surroundings seemed unfamiliar to her, Ms. Davison was excited about her new job and about teaching in a diverse setting. In fact, Ms. Davison had been hired specifically because of her interest in diversity. Her graduate thesis had been on culture and music learning, and she graduated at the top of her class from a program that focused on social justice and culturally responsive teaching.

Ms. Davison was visiting her new classroom during her summer break with plans to arrange the room and choose the literature for her first concert. She entered the room and was struck by how familiar it seemed. The posters on the walls were the exact same ones she had seen while student teaching and the music in the folders were familiar titles from her days as a high school student. As she continued to look around the room, she was disheartened to realize there was very little that connected the classroom to the community. She knew she had her work cut out for her and she began making plans to spend her summer getting to know the community and learning as much about her students as possible.

Reflective prompt: We often talk about how important it is to get to know our students, but as a new teacher you have to make plans before the first class period. What can Ms. Davison do over the summer to help her better understand her students? What information will best help her plan lessons that are both relevant and applicable?

In Their Own Words: Perspectives on Music Education

In Chapter 4, we identified religious and social groups, close relatives, neighbors, and other significant members of society as crucially important to a child's growth and development. We have begun to recognize the important role society plays in education and tapping into the culture of the community has become a key component to culturally responsive teaching. As John stated:

> the teacher needs to know something about the community they teach in so that they can, first and foremost, connect with the musical experiences the students have through their own cultures; kind of use those connections in their teaching. Use what the students are good at—because of what they do in their own cultures—as part of their lessons.

Getting to know the community is important but recognizing that student and family norms may not connect to the immediate community is an important consideration. Petra's mother chose to send her child to a school three hours away from their family home to a school in a safer neighborhood. However, there was a disconnect between the culture of the community and that of this immigrant household several miles away.

> Definitely, when I was in school my teachers would ask me, "Why don't more students like you take more AP classes or honors classes?" And I would ask myself, "Yeah, why is that?" I would also ask myself as well, "Why aren't there Brown kids in the principal positions in the orchestra? Why do I have to behave a different way, talk a different way when I'm in an educational setting?" In context by the way, I would have to go really far to my grade school because the other schools in my area weren't that great, so it was like a different cultural dynamic.

Allen is an excellent example of a teacher who recognized the value of what his students brought to the classroom. He described how he changed his entire concept of what school music programs could be, based on what he saw his students accomplishing outside of the school building.

> [Y]ou know, my kids would come to me and say, "We have a gig at this church on Friday" and this would be my jazz ensembles. [I said] "Did you book this yourself?" And they said, "Yeah, they heard us play at the other place and they want us to come play for the Strawberry Festival." And I'd say, "What do you need?" They'd say, "We need the PA system, we need the drum set, we need the bass, we need this stuff." I'm like, "Do you need me there?" And they said, "No we got this." And I'm like—success! … [My students were developing] independent musicianship. And those are kids that are still playing because they understand how to set up the PA system, they understand how to do that.

In writing about learning that endures over time, Wiggins and McTighe (2005) stress the importance of developing lessons that have value beyond the classroom and Allen has done just that. He saw that his students were contributing to their community, and he wanted to support their work. He began to focus on facilitating rather than directing. Brielle likewise recognized the value of working with student learning goals, knowing that her students were part of a larger music scene.

> I always have parents and students come in and they say they already have a goal set: "I would like to play for my church choir … I would like to sing at such and such." Sometimes … we are so caught in our little space that we forget that we're impacting the lives of not only our children, but the community.

In some ways, music teachers face a unique challenge when connecting music in school to the community. Music is intricately tied to human identity, and many children first experience music as part of their religious ceremonies. The music they sing in those ceremonies is foundational to their musicianship. Connecting to ceremonial music can be valuable in bridging the community and school but singing religious music in school is a sensitive issue for music teachers. As Tim Drummond pointed out in his article "Singing over the Wall: Legal and Ethical Considerations for Sacred Music in Schools" (2014), music teachers often find themselves caught in the middle of two opposing views about religious music in schools. "Swing too far in either direction, and you're likely to be the hot topic at your next school board meeting for either 'religious indoctrination' or fueling a 'war on Christmas'" (Drummond, 2014, p. 27). Drummond provides valuable information for teachers concerned about the First Amendment by highlighting the legal findings from the 1971 court case *Lemon v. Kurtzman*. The court ruled that sacred music in schools must fulfill three requirements.

1. It must have a secular purpose.
2. It must have a primary effect that neither enhances nor inhibits religion.
3. It must not "foster an excessive government entanglement with religion"
   Lemon v. Kurtzman, *1971, as cited in Drummond, 2014*

In Drummond's article, the author outlined a culturally responsive approach to using sacred music in schools and highlighted culturally responsive practices:

> Indeed, teachers may find a valuable link to their students and the community by embracing cultural traditions in their music-making. A teacher in a school with a large population of Armenian students would definitely want to highlight music and performance practices from that culture,

perhaps even bringing in parents or other local residents as special musical presenters. The same is true in a school with large numbers of adherents to a particular religion; we are wise to acknowledge and celebrate the musical traditions of our students.

(Drummond, 2014, p. 29)

Drawing upon Community Expertise

Vignette

Mr. Medina teaches instrumental music in Southern California where approximately 65% of his students are Hispanic. Three years ago, Mr. Medina was approached by a new student who had just emigrated from Veracruz, Mexico with his family. The student asked Mr. Medina if he could start a mariachi band. Mr. Medina was excited about the possibility, but he had never played with a mariachi group and he did not feel prepared to direct such an ensemble. He did, however, have a close friend who played the *guitarron* for a local group. He immediately called the friend and asked for help.

Mr. Medina got more than he bargained for. During the first planning meeting, the entire mariachi group showed up and together with the student from Veracruz, they developed a plan for an afterschool program. The community group helped with song charts and attended a few of the early rehearsals. They even helped the students raise money to buy instruments and a set of *trajes de charro*, the traditional clothing of mariachi ensembles. By the end of the first year, the student group was ready for their first public performance and they participated in the spring concert along with the school band and orchestra.

The response to the performance was overwhelming. Family members crowded the auditorium and when the student mariachi group took the stage, the energy of the audience was electrifying. While mariachi was new to some of the audience members, many of the parents and grandparents recognized songs from their youth and gleamed with pride as they listened to the familiar melodies. It was clear that something special was happening as the audience cheered and applauded the final song of the evening.

Reflective prompt: Often, teachers only include music in their curriculum that they are familiar with or that they are comfortable performing or teaching. What resources are available to music teachers wanting to support their students' learning goals in areas outside of their expertise?

In Their Own Words: Perspectives on Music Education

Lena discovered a valuable resource within her own family and was able to draw upon the expertise of her husband.

> *When we were married, he would help a lot with Japanese language, because I have a lot of Japanese American students here. He recorded a Seesaw [app for communicating with students and families] message for one of my kids last fall. The student was super shy. His mom had written a note [saying], "too shy to sing on the recording" but [the student] found a link to his favorite song and sent it to me, and so my ex-husband recorded a message in Japanese to send back to the student, and it just made all the difference. This kid sings in class now.*

By drawing upon the husband's knowledge of the Japanese language, this teacher was able to make a connection that impacted the student's ability to participate in music-making.

Unfortunately, we do not all have family members with the expertise we need at any given moment. Stew recognized the importance of knowing the community, and as a pre-service music education student he identified this as a primary area of concern.

> *One of the biggest barriers is not being a part of the culture I'm trying to accommodate in my classroom. So there's going to be a lot of research involved, and a lot of community outreach is going to be necessary and really trying to bridge the gap between the community and the program inside the classroom. I think my lack of experience, … I'm not sure how to organize that, develop that, I'm not sure how to organize all that I do, recognize the importance of it and really trying to bring the culture that already exists into the classroom and not try to fabricate it or create it from myself. So, acknowledging and utilizing those external culture bearers in the community that already exist.*

It is impossible for any of us to be experts in every type of music, and community members can be valuable assets when exploring music outside of our expertise. John described how he was able to draw upon his community members when developing lessons for his elementary music classes.

> *I try to find a culture bearer … If it is a student, fine. Sometimes too, especially in third, fourth, and fifth grade, they are a little embarrassed to ask, so if I can find an adult in the community—I send out these group emails to my school faculty and staff to see if anyone knows anyone—we are singing the Birch Tree, so I asked if anyone might have knowledge of balalaika. I try to search the community.*

John also described how, as a teacher in a diverse community, he was not just concerned with what music to teach; he was also interested in how music learning occurred in diverse cultures.

> *This means I teach music literacy as something much broader than interpreting symbols from a page. When I'm teaching a song from a certain tradition, I also think about how one would learn that song in that tradition. Then, I think about my teaching situation and my students. How does what my students are used to (in terms of learning a song) compare to how the song would be taught in its original culture? Is there some overlap? What method or mixture of methods would give my students the best experience with this song?*

McAlister (2013, p. 1) reported that one of the most important resources community groups can bring to a school is a "deep knowledge of community context and history." Lloyd tapped into his community expertise when working on the musical *Fiddler on the Roof*. He described how bringing cultural insiders into the classroom when working on the musical positively impacted his students' learning and left a lasting impression on all those involved.

> *I'll never be as authentic as a person from that culture … If you can bring in, have authenticism, that always resonates with kids. We did* Fiddler on the Roof *a couple years ago and actually had a Jewish parent who—I think her parents had lived in a village very similar to the one in* Fiddler on the Roof*—had experienced klezmer music. The parent came in with a slide presentation and could talk so specifically about the very issues we were trying to get our heads wrapped around with the show in ways that I could never do, even if I'd read the right books. I could never talk about it with the kind of personal connections and stories they brought to it. For the kids, I think it really resonated and it sticks with them more than just me telling them one more time.*

The community members were better able to present a bigger picture of what life was like for the characters in the musical and they provided valuable background information on the plot.

Hess (2019) offers a few important caveats about making use of the musical expertise of community cultural insiders in schools. When only one representative of a specific cultural group is invited to share their knowledge, the potential for stereotyping is present, not to mention the implication that the person is representing everyone in their culture, a role that people from marginalized populations are far too familiar with. Hess also questions the use of the term "culture bearer" because it suggests that only certain individuals or groups have "culture" and on a more covert level "implies that White individuals lack culture, as music education culture bearers typically consist of people of color" (2019, p. 133). To avoid these problematic issues, Hess suggests using multiple insiders from a given culture to emphasize that a variety of perspectives and facets of expertise exist within one culture, which can go a long way toward diminishing the tendency toward stereotyping.

Cheryl also drew upon the community to enrich her students' learning. With the goal of providing role models for her male students, Cheryl began to invite adult male teachers into her classroom to sing. She wanted her boys to see men participating in a choir.

> *I'm a female teacher, and modeling for boys is always a little bit of a challenge. I'm looking for a way to get men into the choir to model for them—even if it's only for a short time. So, in my men's chorus, I was having the eighth graders model for the fifth and sixth grades, especially during the voice change … so once we started that, I was looking for adult men. I'd ask around, I'd see if I could get some male teachers to come in and sing, even if it was just a one-time thing.*

She realized the benefit of having adult male role models in the choir and began to invite other male singers to join her choir, eventually creating an intergenerational men's choir.

> *That kind of led me to think about inviting community members in general to join us full time. I started to spread the word, I emailed the school district to try and get all of the men in the district if they were interested, and that led to a few teachers joining the group. We sort of passed it around, word of mouth and I emailed parents. We did a newspaper article about it, so I got some adult males. [They were] mostly parents, grandparents and some retirees from the community who were available on Friday afternoons at 3:00.*

Cheryl described how both the community members and her students benefited from their participation in the choir.

> *It's been cool for the adult men who have never had this opportunity. Some of them haven't sung in a long time, and some of them maybe never sang before, and now they get to. And it lets them create a connection with the youth that they wouldn't already have. For my students, beyond the vocal modeling, it is really more about the boys seeing adult men singing; [to see] it's a cool thing to do, it's an acceptable or normal thing to do. This is that special age when the kids get to be self-conscious and unfortunately our society doesn't have the best view of male singers. I wanted our middle school boys to see that adult men, functioning adult men that are contributing to society also enjoy singing and have enjoyed singing.*

Working with community partners can have a lasting effect on community members, teachers, and students, though not all lessons are positive. Claire described how she learned a valuable lesson on her first attempt to expose her students to advanced string players.

> *I discovered … I made a mistake in my first year of teaching. I had a friend of mine who had private students and I had them come to the school. And they all came with their velvet cases and their golden hair and their Bach. And my students just looked like … "what?" you know. It didn't help them at all. And as I started to research, I realized, gosh, I need to give my kids role models, I need to give them people who look like themselves; they need to see people playing in the orchestra. I've seen students go see the symphony (this is nothing against our symphony at all), this is typical—they go with great excitement, and I watch them sit on the edge of the chair, and they look across the stage, and then I see them sit back. And of course, I know what's happened.*

Claire quickly realized that her students couldn't connect with the students she invited into her classroom. She worked to find a better community connection and her efforts paid off.

> *And so I learned of the work of the Sphinx organization and three years ago we brought in the all Black and Latino orchestra to the _____ County Schools for a residency and made the tickets affordable so that families could go to the concerts— we've carried on that tradition now for the last two years … the kids still talk about it. There were so many pieces to that. After the concert, we actually had a workshop at the cultural arts center on a Saturday morning for high school kids. I didn't know who would come. We actually had 75 students come. Most of them never took private lessons. They came on a Saturday morning and spent three hours working with the musicians from the [Sphinx] orchestra. It was just amazing.*

It's not surprising that Claire's students reacted positively to musicians who reflected their own cultural background. Research indicates students are more likely to identify with adults who are from similar backgrounds and who are the same gender and ethnicity (Hamann & Walker, 1993). By tapping into a community of African American and Latino string players, Claire was able to show her students what was possible.

Bringing the community into the classroom can be rewarding and often has unexpected results. Leonora described how a single connection to someone in her community made a big impact on her fourth-grade class. A fellow musician and friend approached Leonora and expressed an interest in doing a composition project with the elementary students.

> *[Her colleague said] "You know, I would like to do a songwriting project with you and your students." And she said, "Well, do you have a special ensemble?" I said, "No, I just have, you know, teach my classes or whatever." And she said, "Well, you*

know, I'm dabbling in composing and I just thought it would be great if kids could see that they can write music if they have musical ideas, if they could bring words together, they get a little melody in their head or whatever. It can actually become a song." And I said, "You know what, I would be happy to help you with this and I know the group that we are going to do it with." And I told her we're going to do it with my most difficult grade-level, the fourth grade. We would do that in lieu of learning recorders. And she said, "Oh, OK!" She didn't know what she was getting into … what we started with was just the process of what they thought about singing and music in general. And each session we would have, we would have them initially give individual ideas, and then come together and work together.

Leonora continued by describing how this project made a lasting impression on the class, motivating them to learn more about music and drastically improving the classroom environment.

Claire has immersed herself in African American culture, researching the history of her area and attending community events. At one such event, she met a spoken word artist and began collaborating with him. Although she admitted to feeling awkward when she was the "only White person" around, she is committed to learning about her students' lives and growing in her understanding of the culture that surrounds her.

And so this would mean rehearsing and going to their house to rehearse and to be honest, I've never been—I had friends that were African American but I've never been like the only White person in a house where everybody else was Black and not me. So it was just, you know, you're just [by] yourself, you know, why haven't I done this before and why is that, and just realizing it's—it's a very interesting experience. And then we would do shows and some of the shows—spoken word is a very upright, in-your-face type of art form and it would be very interesting just to hear where people were coming from—what they were thinking, and sometimes, even their poetry was not really favorable towards blond-headed—specifically saying things about blond-headed, blue eyed people and I'm going, "OK."

Several people we interviewed described the challenges of bringing the community into the classroom. Lena described how one of her Mexican American students approached her and described her desire to play piano.

She had said it a couple different times and I [said] "okay cool, let me help you with that" and her kindergarten teacher asked, "Can you help us find a bilingual teacher?" So, I started texting with a mom in Spanish, figured out that we had found a teacher who would teach in Spanish, but the family didn't have an instrument. I emailed the principal and asked, "Can they come to the school to use the piano?" He said no, just because it was too much of a hassle with Covid and the locking and unlocking [of the building]. I thought, you do not understand all of the groundwork that was

> *just laid to make this happen. And this might … [be an opportunity for the student].*
> *And now, this girl cannot play piano. So I think he gets it but doesn't get it, if that*
> *makes sense.*

Lena's principal missed an opportunity to connect with the community and support learning outside of the classroom.

Massimo likewise described a barrier to bringing the community into the classroom. Massimo often works with hip-hop in his general music classes and he invites local musicians to speak to his classes. He pointed out the need to "warn" the front office when certain musicians were invited to the school.

> *When two African American women would check into the building, too young, fierce,*
> *black women walking in, I would have to warn our front office—hey I'm expecting*
> *these guests because the first time I didn't do that it set off a whole bunch of protocol*
> *… I just gotta say—if it was two White men, it wouldn't have been an issue.*

Working to bring the community into the classroom certainly has its challenges and many schools are not prepared to open their doors to diverse music makers. Luis described how teaching during Covid made it somewhat easier to bring the community into the classroom.

> *I am able to show kids things that I wouldn't have before. I brought a friend of mine*
> *who is a drag queen, and she sings and she's a performer and she dances. I [said*
> *to her], "What if you just did a [30-minute set]? You can sing some songs, talk*
> *about the songs, you could dance, and I think the kids would love it." They would*
> *see a performer, it'd be maybe someone different that they haven't seen before, and*
> *I was really interested to see what the kids' reaction would be. They looked at her as*
> *I would think they would look at a clown which is great, because she had all these*
> *costumes [and] props and she had a lot of makeup on. And this one kid [in] third*
> *grade [said], "Are your eyelashes real?" and [she said], "Yes, they are"—they were*
> *this big [uses his fingers to simulate eyelashes]. And [the student said], "You must be*
> *so old because your eyelashes are really long!" and she [said], "Maybe!" and I had*
> *to cover my camera [so the students wouldn't see him laughing]. And I don't know if*
> *she would have been able to come to the school and do a performance in regular time*
> *but that was something! [I thought] "Wow, how cool." She was able to perform for*
> *these kids in the middle of the school day and things like that, I'm grateful for being*
> *able to, because of Covid, be able to have performances and things that we wouldn't*
> *have been able to do.*

Throughout our interviews, we heard about the value of connecting the classroom with the community, but as Claire stated, "the reality is, it isn't always easy." It is challenging to understand the boundaries (and challenge those boundaries when appropriate), be sensitive to diverse populations, and avoid stereotyping or tokenism. Yet Claire, along with many of the people we interviewed, recognized the importance of stepping out of their comfort zones and connecting to the real lived experiences of their students and the people who surround those students. When asked why she continued to put herself in uncomfortable situations, Claire replied,

> *I want to be sensitive and I want to be aware of where people are coming from. You can't fix everything but [you can] at least be aware.*

Learning Outside the School Room

Vignette

For several years, Ms. Davis had taken her choral ensemble on a holiday tour, caroling at a nursing home and at the children's hospital. Ms. Davis had recently begun volunteering at a local homeless shelter and she arranged to have her students sing for the residents during their community tour.

When the bus arrived at the shelter, Ms. Davis asked her students to remain seated while she checked to see if the director was ready for their arrival. As she walked into the cafeteria, she was surprised to see the room filled to capacity with children setting on their parents' laps and a few residents seated on the floor against the wall. One resident sat at the piano playing a jazz tune while another resident played drums on an old drum kit setting in the corner. As she looked around, she noticed a few residents were holding guitars and many were clapping along to the music. She returned to the bus and talked to the students about what she saw in the cafeteria. One of her students exclaimed, "maybe they could sing with us" and the group quickly decided to turn their performance into a "sing-a-long."

The event was nothing like what Ms. Davis had planned, and it turned out to be a life-changing event. The residents sang and played along to the music. Because the room was crowded, the students mingled with the residents. Ms. Davis noticed how comfortable the students were talking with the adults and how eager the adults were to talk to her students. Before leaving, several of the residents asked the students to return and one mentioned a desire to start a choir at the shelter. The talk on the bus ride home was energized and focused. The students wanted to return, and they wanted to start a choir.

Ms. Davis met with the school administration and was given the green light to start an outreach choir at the shelter. She formed a small task force made up of parents, students, and shelter residents. Together, the group decided on goals for the program and they worked to develop a structure that would work for both the students and the shelter staff. Within two weeks, the intergenerational choir was formed. The group began meeting one evening a week and by spring they were ready for their first performance. With help from the shelter staff, they performed for a sold-out audience raising money for the shelter and also donating funds to another community organization. Together, the students and residents of the shelter continue to meet and perform with the overarching goal of changing their community for the better through music.

Reflective prompt: This vignette illustrates how learning can occur outside of the school and how students can make a positive impact on their community. What challenges do you think Ms. Davis faced in taking advantage of this learning opportunity? Why do you think administrators would or would not support such a program?

In Their Own Words: Perspectives on Music Education

The teachers we interviewed diligently looked for ways to connect their students to the community. In Chapter 6, we mentioned how Claire used the history of her school to connect to her students. While researching the elementary school's namesake, Claire also learned about the work of Dr. John Hope Franklin, an African American historian who taught at Duke University for 35 years. Because Claire taught in a school that served a student population that was primarily African American, she wanted to share what she learned about Dr. Franklin with her students.

> *Another cool connection—watched a Ken Burns documentary and learned who John Hope Franklin was and connected with—found that he taught at Duke University (where have I been?) and contacted the center there and told them about our school, told them the [school namesake's] story, and they invited us to come to the John Hope Franklin center and play. When we did that, a couple of weeks, right before going I got brave enough to call the [Duke] chapel and see if we could come in and just open up our cases and hear our sound. And they said yes. So for the last five years now we've been going and not only do we hear our sound, we have a little prepared program that the children play their violins at Duke Chapel and they also sing now, all the children … Oh, and I taught them how the campus was designed by Julian Abele, the first prominent African American architect in our country. And we talked about how he didn't like to come to Duke because of the Jim Crow South and we also talked about the fact that in front of the chapel was a very important demonstration after Martin Luther King died. The [Duke] students were upset because the administration really wasn't acknowledging his death. And so there was … I showed the kids how there was this demonstration, a peaceful one,*

in front of the chapel so when they step on that ground, they understand what's happened before them.

Expanding the learning environment to include venues outside of the classroom can provide unique opportunities for making community connections. James, who has arranged for his students to perform at numerous community venues including veterans' homes, homeless shelters, and homes for abused women and children, talked about how important it was to have his students engage in conversations with the adults they performed with.

> *School bands don't do this sort of thing very often, choirs do—they go out to senior assisted living places during the holidays and such, but bands really don't and not in a homeless shelter. What sets us really apart from others that do go out, is the visitation. Normally a chorus would go out and sing in a senior home and after the concert they will file out and go home. We schedule up to an hour where my kids are instructed to go meet as many people as they can. And I tell them I am going to want them to come into some type of respectful, physical contact. It can be as simple as a handshake. That handshake usually never happens because they end up hugging each other.*

James talked about his focus on cultural and social outreach and how his middle school band (predominantly comprised of Latinx students) has worked to better understand the community and how they have also been a positive presence in his community.

> *We do have marching band, but we do something different than what others are doing. I pick parades that have a cultural theme to it. Since we are in LA County, we are a melting pot of cultures. In Los Angeles, the history is the Latino, Black, and Korean communities have big time gangs, and they kill each other. Every year, we do a Korean Parade and in place of competition, I have my kids do some type of research project about Korea—mostly cultural themes. In groups of four they create poster boards and report back to the group what they learned. When we get to the parade, we surround our band with the Korean National Flag, and the music we play is the Korean National Anthem. We march through Korea town and the crowd is screaming and waving. For Black History Month we do something similar, the kids are assigned a Black hero to research. [When we march in the parade], we put up custom-made flags with the names of Black heroes on them, so the Latino culture is extending a beautiful handshake of peace into the [two cultures that have the biggest conflict].*

Music is unique in that there are many community programs that focus on music learning for youth that operate outside of a formal educational setting, yet these programs impact the schools. Pre-service music student, Petra, described how participating in a youth music project impacted music learning, not just in the community but also at school.

So [my mother] put me in the Harmony Project because she wanted me to be involved in music so I wouldn't be involved in gangs and whatnot. It was a really foundational experience, I think maybe I didn't think of it when I was a student there, maybe I just thought it was a music thing. But now, just thinking about in the moment of my life right now where I'm like what did the past seven years of my life mean, how did that shape who I am now. I'm still trying to decipher that. But it's wonderful. I talked to so many teachers, I engaged in community, I learned how to play an instrument, and I took all of that back to grade school.

Making strong community connections is both a result of and a support for culturally responsive teaching. By finding ways for students to connect in meaningful ways to the community, and by tapping into the expertise of parents, grandparents, neighbors, and friends, music programs can thrive. True community/school partnerships, however, require a committed effort by all parties involved.

Key Considerations for Building School and Community Partnerships

- Relationships matter. Programs that focus on building respectful and trusting relationships among school staff, families, community members, and students are more effective and sustainable.
- Developing good relationships with community members is not always easy. Not all parents have experienced affirming and respectful relationships with schools and it may take time for them to trust you.
- Including administration in the planning and implementation of community–school partnerships helps avoid problems.
- Including parents and community members in decision-making and governance can help build a bridge between school and home.
- Using a variety of forms of communication between home, school, and community ensures that people will be able to participate and can help establish trust.
- Exploring the community around the school can help you learn more about the music culture and better understand your students. Make it a point to visit venues that feature live music and stay informed about community festivals and holiday celebrations.
- Providing learning opportunities in the community can be a way to garner additional support for your program.
- Expanding your definition of "community" can lead to great opportunities for your students. School staff, faculty, and administration often have interests and experiences that relate to your classroom.
- Music faculty from local colleges and universities can be great resources. Many faculty members have developed expertise in specific music genres and are eager to share their love for a specific culture or style. Additionally, service

to the community is required of most tenure track faculty and many will be eager to find meaningful ways to fulfill this requirement.
- Community engagement is strengthened when students interact one-on-one with community members. Teach your students how to introduce themselves to adults and provide them with talking points to engage others in conversation.

Summary

Music teachers are poised to take a leadership role in developing strong community connections. By capitalizing on the positive relationships already established, and by strategically planning to broaden the connection between the music program and the community, music teachers are beautifully situated to improve learning for their students and make a positive impact on society. Epstein et al. (1997) described how community and school partnerships can revitalize a neighborhood, strengthen the family, and increase student achievement. Henderson and Mapp (2002) found that when schools, families, and community groups worked together to support learning, children tended to do better in school, stay in school longer, and generally like school more. The teachers we interviewed echoed these findings and emphasized how working with the community strengthened their teaching and helped them meet the needs of their students.

Discussion Questions

1. Do you think all students, regardless of race or ethnicity, would feel comfortable participating in a culturally specific ensemble?
2. What are some specific ideas you would encourage a music director to use when working to make all students feel welcome in the school ensembles?
3. Other than financially, how can the community support school music programs?
4. What skills and expertise do your community members possess that would be helpful in your school music program?
5. How can we use technology, social media platforms, and video conferencing applications, to strengthen our connections to the community?
6. Throughout this book, we have referenced culturally specific music styles. What are the barriers that music teachers face when including diverse music in their curriculum?
7. Many of the teachers we interviewed described how they had to give up their preconceived ideas of what music education should look like to make more relevant and meaningful curriculum choices for their students. Who has had the biggest impact on your vision of music education? Is your vision relevant to your community?

References

Drummond, T. (2014). Singing over the wall: Legal and ethical considerations for sacred music in schools. *Music Educators Journal, 101*(2), 27–31.

Eby, J. (1998). Why service-learning is bad. *Service Learning, General, 27.* https://digitalcommons.unomaha.edu/slceslgen/27

Epstein, J. L., Simon, B. S., & Salinas, K. C. (1997). Involving parents in homework in the middle grades. *Research Bulletin, 18.* Phi Delta Kappa/Center for Evaluation, Development, and Research.

Garoutte, L., & McCarthy-Gilmore, K. (2014). Preparing students for community-based learning using an asset-based approach. *Journal of the Scholarship of Teaching and Learning, 14*(5), 48–61. http://files.eric.ed.gov/fulltext/EJ1047966.pdf

Gay, G. (2018). *Culturally responsive teaching: Theory, research, and practice* (3rd ed.) Teachers College Press.

Hamann, D., & Walker, L. (1993). Music teachers as role models, *Journal of Research in Music Education, 41*(4), 303–314.

Henderson, A. T., & Mapp, K. L. (2002). *A new wave of evidence: The impact of school, family and community connections on student achievement.* National Center for Family & Community Connections with Schools.

Hess, J. (2019). *Music education for social change: Constructing an activist music education.* Routledge.

McAlister, S. (2013). Why community engagement matters in school turnaround. *Voices in Urban Education, 36,* 35–42.

Wiggins, G., & McTighe, J. (2005). *Understanding by design.* ASCD Publishing.

8

A VISION FOR CULTURALLY RESPONSIVE MUSIC EDUCATION

> Never doubt that a small group of thoughtful, committed, citizens can change the world. Indeed, it is the only thing that ever has.
>
> *Margaret Mead*

What Music Education Can Be

We passionately believe every child has a right to music education. Both of us have spent our careers working towards that goal. We know that music is personal; it is a part of who we are, and it is a part of who our students are. We work and teach in a subject area that is integrated into the human psyche, a subject area that is a rich and vibrant reflection of our humanness. As Jill pointed out in her interview,

> we have so many new Americans, that I think the kids go further when they feel that there is an element of who they are that is present in the school, and they have a role in embracing that during their school day because so much of the school day is unnatural. It is unnatural to study geometry. It's unnatural to have all the things and so I think it's that creativity being so tied to the true self.

Music is one of the most natural things for many of us. It's in our homes, our places of worship, it's a part of our celebrations, and it helps us mourn. While music is an integral part of who we are as humans, there is often a disconnect between the music that we value and the music that we study in school. Culturally responsive teaching in music points to purposes, goals, and objectives for music education that are connected to what students bring to the classroom and have the potential to

DOI: 10.4324/9781003208136-11

transform much of how we "do" music in American schools. If we truly embrace the concepts of culturally responsive teaching, music education will look and feel different than what many of us experienced in schools. It will be different in some ways that we can anticipate and in other ways that we have yet to imagine. In this chapter, we offer our vision of what music education might become (and in some places is becoming) and discuss ways to think about and implement this vision. Because culturally responsive teaching encompasses a mindset and is not a curriculum or set of instructions, our vision may seem vague or idealistic. We ask the reader to consider our vision within the larger scope of "what might be" and imagine music education being transformed from the ground up. We ask that you put aside your pre-existing ideas of what music education looks and sounds like and allow yourself to consider new possibilities by reflecting upon an outcome where music education really is connected to every child, their family, and their community.

First and foremost, we envision a music education process where music teachers intentionally connect what they do in the classroom to the lives of their students. As Claire described, we have to look beyond what we read or what we have been taught and really think about our students.

> You can have all the head knowledge [about culturally responsive teaching], we can talk about this stuff, and hopefully, by people hearing us talk, they'll understand. But there has to be something in your heart that's going to make this a deliberate thing. I think you have to be passionate about it. And the children … if you're passionate, they'll be passionate. If you're passive, they'll be passive. If you're shaming and antagonistic towards them, they'll just show you right back. So you have to really respect that they're people, just like you and I. They're just little people. But they're no less than me—they're just younger "me's" or younger "you's."

Our students come to school music classrooms and rehearsal spaces with years of musical experiences. We know that infants respond to music and even at four years old, children can demonstrate their musicality. Just watch any preschooler at play. They make up songs to accompany whatever they are doing or to express how they feel, and they do it spontaneously, without prompting from adults. They recognize familiar melodies, and they often move in rhythm to the sounds around them. Music education should build upon that inclination and nurture it. Because music is a means of self-expression, we envision students creating their own music, not just interpreting through performance what has already been composed. Our vision of music education corresponds to Small's (1998) idea of "musicking," which he defined as "[taking] part, in any capacity, in a musical performance, whether by performing, by listening, by rehearsing or practicing, by providing material for performance (what is called composing), or by dancing" (p. 9). Giving students the opportunity to express their musicality in a full range of ways can be a powerful experience and can provide teachers with valuable insight into the lives of their students.

A culturally responsive approach to music education means valuing what students already know and finding ways to expand upon that prior knowledge. We are not saying that music education will become exclusively centered on contemporary music practices, nor are we calling for the elimination of Western European classical music performance. Rather, we can use what our students already know about music as the "Doorway-In(to)" (Wiggins, 2015) exploring and experiencing unfamiliar musics. By bringing the music our students are familiar with at home into the classroom, we can build upon an already established foundation for musical understanding.

Our vision of music education is one where the value and importance of lifelong music-making is a central focus of music instruction. To be clear, most, if not all, music teachers would acknowledge this as a primary *goal* of music education; however, the nature of our *instruction* often fails to achieve the goal. According to Regelski (2007), this is due to the (Western) tendency to define musicianship only in terms of the quality of the music being made, rather than by the quality of the *experience* of music-making.

During our interview, Petra stated:

> the arts are really, truly meant to celebrate humanity and music is more or less the same if not more. When you begin to line up, you know there are some systematic issues in play that are not involving you to be in the conversation; it's pretty jarring. When you take away the humanity in art and music, not only do you begin to appropriate it, but you get in the habit of only celebrating the art form itself. I've been under instructors where the entire semester we would be full of rote learning, where we just focus on playing Beethoven, Bach, and Brahms. And I love those composers, don't get me wrong. But when we talk about improving a community, which is what an orchestra is, I don't know, do you expect students to become better people just by playing Beethoven, Brahms, and Bach? You're like zombifying people into thinking these dead composers will make a community better. I think that's pretty silly.

We agree with Petra; not only is it silly, but this approach to music education hinders students from fully realizing their musicianship. Regelski proposed that if music educators reclaim the responsibility to develop "amateur" musicians, we will be better able to connect to our students' potential. In this case, Regelski is choosing the definition of "amateur" as one who engages in an activity for pleasure rather than for financial compensation and not the alternative definition of one who is unskilled at a task. The development of amateur musicians is achieved by encouraging music-making by all rather than by a select few. Indeed, many of our students come from cultures where music-making is a communal activity in which everyone is expected to participate because everyone has something to contribute. The music education we envision does not privilege only those students who exhibit extraordinary talent within Western classical musical forms. Rather, it offers learners the opportunity to engage in a broad spectrum of musical traditions, forms, and performance practices that highlight the potential for making and engaging with music throughout their lives.

Our vision for music education is one where our students enthusiastically participate because the class connects in a deep and meaningful way to their identity and to their values. Culturally responsive teaching calls us as music educators to learn who our students are musically as well as individually and to assist them in achieving their musical goals. We envision music education taking place in such a way that what happens in the individual school music classroom and rehearsal space is specific to the needs, desires, and aspirations of the students inhabiting them. This vision requires teachers to make decisions thoughtfully and intentionally in response to what they know about their students, what they understand about the families they serve, and what they know about what it means to be musical. It is not simply adding on a few new "pop" songs or incorporating "world music." Rather, it involves infusing the ideals of culturally responsive teaching into every aspect of the classroom.

Reactive versus Proactive Change

Engendering change is challenging. It is challenging because change requires us to step outside of our comfort zones. Changes in educational institutions and systems frequently take a long time because they involve groups of people being able to tolerate the discomfort of the unknown and the unfamiliar. Considering giving up what we are comfortable with runs against our natural inclinations toward the assurance, security, and sometimes the rewards associated with doing "what we have always done."

But sometimes, circumstances occur that demand change, whether we are ready for it or not. The onslaught of the coronavirus pandemic is just such a circumstance. The impact of the pandemic has been far-reaching, and essentially has changed the nature of how instruction occurs. Across the United States, teachers had only days to shift from face-to-face to online instruction. The ease of accommodating this shift differed depending on instructional setting, and district and state educational agencies. Social media pages sprang up overnight where teachers sought advice and support from one another as they navigated daily changes in information about how best to meet the challenges posed by the virus. The constraints that the pandemic placed on live music-making was one of the most difficult challenges, one that forced music educators to find alternate ways to engage students in music-making, much of it occurring virtually. Teachers learned more about the benefits and limitations of computer technology and expanded their notions of what music teaching and learning could look and sound like.

At the same time, concerns regarding the status of racial justice in the U.S. hit a tipping point with the murder of George Floyd. The death of Floyd prompted global protests and was a critical point in the Black Lives Matter movement, which had been drawing national attention to the number of deaths of unarmed Black men and women and other people of color at the hands of the police. The term "systemic racism" was articulated and debated in national media in ways that heretofore had not been possible or probable. By the start of Fall 2020, often at the behest of students and communities, faculty at primary, secondary, and tertiary levels of education were analyzing curricula to determine how they could more meaningfully reflect the cultural content knowledge and skills of diverse socio-cultural groups.

These events are apt examples of reactive change. In the case of Covid-19, the deadly consequences of contracting the virus necessitated immediate response; decisions had to be made quickly based on the best medical information available at the time. Because educational institutions had not dealt with this kind of medical emergency since the polio epidemic of the 1950s, there were not many policies in place that dealt specifically with this kind of threat. The worldwide racial reckoning that accompanied the murder of George Floyd forced into sharp relief issues relating to what many had long identified as institutional, structural, and/or systemic racism, but which had never been discussed on such a large scale. Although the dialogue about curricular change and the actual curricular changes that have occurred did not happen with the same immediacy as the changes that occurred due to Covid-19, one might argue that it still took a significant event to instigate and propel the potential for change.

It is clear that, as mentioned earlier, our tendency toward the familiar and comfortable means that we often do not make changes unless we are forced to in reaction to consequential circumstances. Certainly, reactive change may allow us to see possibilities that were not previously within our view. This has certainly been the case in the examples we provided above. But reactive change, though often necessary, and sometimes positive, is not always the best or most constructive means to effect change that is lasting. Substantive change often requires careful thought and reflection. It also requires a catalyst sufficient to generate the forward momentum needed for change.

What, then, would actually be a sufficient catalyst for change in music education? One motivation for change is recognizing the negative consequences of maintaining the status quo and identifying what we risk for our students by not changing. Several ongoing issues associated with PreK–12 music education are symptomatic of the need for a change in how we view the role of music education, the way we deliver music to our students, and how we represent the value of music education to others.

One issue of concern is the persistent focus on non-musical rationales within our music education advocacy message to the exclusions of articulating music's unique benefits. This tendency is extremely problematic for several reasons. First, for nearly every non-musical benefit attributed to music study and participation (e.g., fostering discipline and *esprit de corps*, developing a sense of achievement, promoting emotional development, and the development of spatial intelligence) there is another activity or endeavor that could provide that same benefit equally well, if not better. Additionally, emphasizing the non-musical benefits of school music might appear to be the way to promote the value of music education in an era of high-stakes testing and calls for teacher accountability, but there can be disadvantages to hitching our wagon to that star. When decisions are made to cut programs based on budgetary needs, how much security does the music education program have if its value lies only in its capacity to provide the same benefits as other subjects and activities? We understand the strategic reasons that drive our profession's emphasis on the non-musical benefits of music, but we believe that the focus has been to the exclusion of the unique music-specific benefits.

Another trend that seems to be exacerbated by our adherence to the status quo in music education is the low enrollment in school music programs of students comprising ethnic and racial minorities. An often-cited reason for the low enrollments is a sense among many students at the middle and high school level that school music is not "real" music and is not relevant to their musical lives outside of school. Limits in the types of ensembles available for students at the middle and high school level also contribute to enrollment declines. "Whether we are aware or not, music educators are sending messages to students and society about what music is, what a musician is, and how people should interact with music" (Bledsoe, 2015, p. 21). For too many students, that message is that the music that interests them and their ways of music-making have no place in the school music curriculum. Small (1998, p. 212) described the following as a "hidden logical chain" underlying some musical practice:

1. Our music (which may be classical music, marching band music, show band music, choral music, or big band jazz but rarely improvised or self-composed music, which is difficult to control) is the only real music.
2. You do not like or are not proficient in or are not interested in our music.
3. Therefore, you are not musical.

Even among those students who are identified as "musical" and participate in traditional performing ensembles, particularly instrumental ensembles, graduation often signals the last time they play their instruments; music performing is replaced by other pursuits.

While we often tout music's value in fostering creative thinking, and recognize creating as an important musical behavior, we do not always provide learners with opportunities to create and manipulate sound in our school music classrooms and rehearsal spaces. This is true despite the fact that our profession has established creating as Anchor Standard #1 among the National Core Music Standards (National Coalition for Core Arts Standards, 2014). Many teachers are not comfortable with teaching students to compose, improvise, or even arrange music; others feel they do not have the time to devote to it during a class period; and still others do not know where to begin. The most common reason, however, that students do not get more experience with organizing musical sound is that our traditional model of music education has never really emphasized this musical behavior, at least not at the secondary levels of education. If we compare music education to education in visual art, the point becomes clear. In most art classes, students have the opportunity to create an object; something new that did not exist before, and which typically represents concepts they have learned through the process of creating within a specific medium. The artifact is a culmination of a creative effort, and it is the experience of creating that is significant. Traditional music education instruction at secondary levels does not often allow students to explore, manipulate, and organize sounds in a way that results in a new aural product, or which gives them the chance to create music "in the moment" through improvisation. Rather, we conduct rehearsals so that students realize our (the director's) interpretation. The students in our music classes may have lots of musical ideas, but they seldom get a chance to try them out. If we insist that they can only create particular types of music in particular ways, then we take away the capacity for the kind of meaningful engagement with music that we claim we want for our students.

Finally, there is the issue of a lack of diversity in our music teaching force. This trend is also reflected in terms of the general PreK–12 teaching population, which, as we indicated in Chapter 2, is primarily White, female, and middle class. Because our traditional model of music education and music teacher education privileges those who are proficient in the music of the Western European classical tradition, musicians who are proficient in other musical forms are excluded from the pool of potential music teacher candidates because there is a disconnect between their music and school music. Additionally, if sociocultural and socioeconomic factors limit who has access to the study of music that is required for entry into music teacher preparation programs, then our teaching force will remain culturally and musically homogeneous, while the cultural backgrounds of our school student populations and their musical tastes continue to be diverse.

The issues highlighted above suggest that we cannot afford to continue following the same model of music education content and delivery first established in America more than a century ago without risking significant negative consequences. American novelist James Baldwin said, "Not everything that is faced can be changed; but nothing can be changed until it is faced" (1962, p. BR11). Thus, the question we ask is, are we ready to face the changes needed to re-envision music education?

Disrupting the Self-Perpetuating Cycle

Change will not come easily; education is multifaceted and, at times, messy. At the root of the challenge is a self-perpetuating cycle that allows the current, traditional model of PreK–12 music education content and delivery to maintain its stronghold (see Figure 8.1). To loosen the exclusionary grip of tradition and allow a new paradigm to be nurtured, we must find a way to interrupt the cycle, to shake us out of our comfort zone.

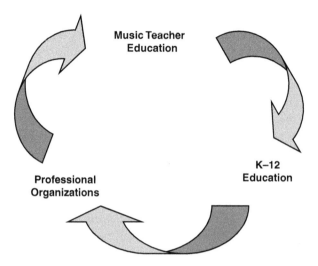

FIGURE 8.1 Illustration of self-perpetuating cycle hindering change in music education

Let's begin by examining the gateway or entry point to music teacher preparation and look carefully at who is being accepted into music teacher education programs. For the most part, first-year applicants are recent graduates from traditional high school music programs who were successful in choir, band, or orchestra. Students proficient in different music traditions who want to become music educators often have difficulty just getting in the door. Entrance exams and auditions in most music teacher education programs are rooted in Western European classical performance practices and proficiencies. Students are expected to perform music that falls within a very narrow range, and those who most closely adhere to that criterion are rewarded with both entrance into the academic institution and scholarship money to support them as they matriculate. Because many music teacher education programs do not have a mechanism for accepting and working with students whose ways of knowing music are different, they serve as a gatekeeper, restricting access to the profession.

How music teacher education programs are accredited is also partially responsible for maintaining Western European classical traditions. The National Association of Schools of Music (NASM), the accrediting agent for many schools of music, requires that students admitted to undergraduate degrees in music demonstrate the ability to "relate musical sound to notation" and must understand music terminology (National Association of Schools of Music, 2021, p. 92). These requirements assume grounding in Western European classical music traditions and exclude anyone who has learned music solely through other traditions. Once admitted, students are further enculturated into a system that favors Western European classical music traditions with private study on a major instrument (voice, woodwind, strings, percussion, keyboard, or brass) and participation in large ensembles (i.e., concert choir, wind ensemble, or orchestra) required. The NASM has called for change by requiring music education students to have experience in composing and arranging, and by requiring world music be included in undergraduate programs, but these requirements fall short of fostering substantive change.

In "Conceptually Framing Music Teaching and Learning within the Context of Culture: Implications for Music Education" (McKoy et al., 2009), we described how this "add-on" model was insufficient to effect change and we cited the prevailing approach to music teacher preparation (an approach where learning is compartmentalized) as one of the problems we face as a profession. Because our students study music theory, music history, pedagogy, and music-making in isolation, they often have difficulty "making connections between what they are studying and how they will teach" (McKoy et al., 2009, p. 62). Our concern has been echoed by Sarath, Myers, and Campbell (2017, p. 58) who have cited the "fragmentation of subjects and skills" as a core deficiency in the current model of music education.

Moving beyond this fragmentation and facilitating a coherent approach to undergraduate music teacher education is not an easy task, but it is one that we believe will help interrupt the self-perpetuating cycle mentioned earlier. Villegas and Lucas (2002, p. 197) pointed out that, to create a conceptually coherent curriculum, we must first "articulate a vision of the role of schools, and the process of teaching and learning in a multicultural society." Creating this cohesive vision and implementing curriculum reform will require critical discourse among all faculty members.

> Engaging our colleagues in discussions about curricular reform with sensitivity and respect is vital to effecting meaningful change. Working within and across departments of music, music education, and general education to complete an honest appraisal of the music education curriculum is a necessary first step. Initiating changes that challenge traditional content and teaching approaches within the university setting can also be an intimidating task. Ongoing discussion regarding the purposes of music education, the nature of the teaching and learning process, which music should be the primary focus of study, the extent of our students' musical knowledge, and the role of music in the school and community will be invaluable in restructuring our curricula in music education to help prepare music teachers who are culturally responsive.
>
> *(McKoy et al., 2009, pp. 62–63)*

Exploring transformation through the lens of culturally responsive teaching must be approached with sensitivity, but by having open and honest discussions about where we need to go as a profession, faculty will be better able to understand the limitations of the current model and they may be more open to reform.

When we mention curriculum reform, we are talking about a complete overhaul of the system. As we stated previously, "add-on courses, one-time field experiences, or superficial 'exposure' to diversity are not sufficient" (McKoy et al., 2009, p. 63). Sarath et al. (2017) recommended the undergraduate curriculum be streamlined to provide room to give students more choices. By creating an "option-rich" framework for undergraduate music study, students are more likely to be engaged in the process and they may be able to better connect learning to personal growth. Additionally, an "option-rich" curriculum allows faculty more creativity in designing and implementing courses and may lead to a more integrated approach to music study.

Alongside a call for more student choice, Sarath et al. (2017) recommended that college and university music schools and departments develop new courses and degree programs that reflect 21st-century needs by focusing on creativity-based, diverse, and integrative practices. We suggest that when creating new courses and/ or making changes to existing programs, it is vitally important to consider ways to integrate the concepts of culturally responsive teaching. It is not only about what is taught but also about how the content is delivered. "We tend to teach as we have been taught; therefore, if we want our students to become culturally responsive teachers, we must show them how" (McKoy et al., 2009, p.63). Undergraduate students must see faculty members engage in music and music learning in new ways and they must believe that these new ways are valid and valued.

The changes we are calling for cannot happen in the "silo" of higher education; rather, it will require change among several entities involved with music study. This takes us to the second cell in our self-perpetuating model: professional organizations. Accrediting agencies (i.e., NASM, CAEP), professional organizations (i.e., National Association for Music Education, American Choral Directors Association, American String Teachers Association, American School Band Directors Association, State Education Agency Directors of Arts Education), and the administrative infrastructure of PreK–12 education act to influence music education. As Sarath et al. (2017) pointed out, collegiate music programs will only be able to implement large-scale reform if there is a simultaneous change in accreditation policies and practices. The involvement of state agencies and PreK–12 administrators in the transformation of music teacher education is also imperative. Upon graduation, most of our students who want to teach in PreK–12 education will be required to pass a standardized test for licensure, a test that is currently biased towards the canon of Western European classical music. Additionally, the students who achieve a degree and are licensed to teach will most likely be hired to oversee traditional music programs. Once hired, new music teachers quickly come to recognize the types of music activities that are accepted and rewarded by their administration and by their professional peers, and they often establish program goals and objectives that align with those activities.

As a whole, professional organizations are an influential force in maintaining the status quo. What is valued and, in many ways, what is rewarded are programs that excel at the familiar. Administrators (often prompted by the music educator) publicly recognize their music programs by highlighting their success at marching competitions and/or music festivals. Likewise, ensemble directors line their shelves with trophies and certificates proclaiming they are "winners." The accolades are not without their value, but we ask you to consider the ramifications of a system so dependent upon this model: who has won, and at what cost? Festival and contest ratings, marching competitions, and state performance assessments are founded on conformity to a single musical standard, and because that standard is associated largely with only one musical tradition, the assessments fail to support innovative, alternative, or global music practices. Peruse any state-approved music list and you will quickly notice a predominance of standard Western European classical music. Certainly, the lists have been expanding over recent years and directors have more choices than before but, for the most part, the approach has been to "add on" one or two different styles or genres, while still maintaining the traditional "core." This tacitly suggests a musical hierarchy, atop which sits music of the Western European classical canon.

Moving the profession towards a more culturally responsive approach to music education is a daunting task, but failure to do so will have long-term negative consequences particularly for those most directly impacted by our choices: PreK–12 music students. This population makes up the final cell in our three-celled model and refers to the students who participate in school music. While music programs in elementary schools typically serve the entire student population, music participation falls away during the middle and high school years except for those students who elect to take band, chorus, or orchestra. Figures differ depending upon the source of the information, but approximately 10% to 20% of high school students are engaged in school music programs. Many of these students find success in school music and decide to major in music at the university level. Students who have participated in traditional programs (and who have excelled in a model that reflects the status quo) are likely to meet entrance requirements for undergraduate music study and will be admitted. Many of these students, already biased toward the current model, will be the students who find success in undergraduate music education, achieve licensure, and will then be hired to teach the next generation of music students. Unless wholesale change is implemented, the cycle will continue.

Interrupting the cycle at the PreK–12 level will involve a paradigm shift in public school music. By engaging students creatively in the act of music-making, and by providing them with several viable paths to music study that align more closely to interests outside of school, we can revitalize the system and provide music instruction for a broader proportion of the student body. Hopefully, some of the students who participate in new models of music instruction at the high school level will become music teachers who will be able and willing to bring a new perspective to PreK–12 classrooms. To facilitate this change, however, there must be a conversation among higher education faculty and PreK–12 music teachers focused specifically on ways to support non-traditional approaches to music study. Students enrolled in courses that reflect a new paradigm at the middle and high school level must have an entrance point into music study at the collegiate level, and once there, must have options that support their continued growth as musicians.

Changing the environment will also require that we include administrators, members of professional organizations, and lawmakers in the conversation. These stakeholders are the ones with the power to approve curricular changes and with the mechanism to provide the necessary professional development supportive of the changes. Support from higher education administrators and lawmakers must be garnered to ensure that the requirements for matriculation, graduation, and licensure align with new standards.

Conclusion

Our respective music teaching experiences over recent years have led us to the conclusion that a culturally responsive approach to music education can transform music learning in significant and meaningful ways. We have seen this in classrooms across the country and we have experienced it in our own teaching. As the epigraph to this chapter states, the efforts of a "small group of thoughtful, committed, citizens can change the world" and for many students, their world has been changed by the thoughtful work of teachers who have embraced culturally responsive teaching.

We hope that this book will serve as a catalyst for continued change among classroom teachers, pre-service undergraduate students, and faculty members involved in music education. We ask that you question your experiences and spend time reflecting upon who you will be teaching. Who is music for? How will you reach out to all students? How is your image of music education limited by your past experiences? How can you broaden your views? Seek out faculty members and/or professional colleagues who share your interests and learn from them and do not limit your music learning to what you may have gained in your respective undergraduate and graduate institutions. Explore your community and find new ways to demonstrate your musicianship.

This text is also written for university faculty wanting to learn more about culturally responsive teaching. We believe it will be useful as a starting point for the conversations that need to take place in faculty meetings in higher education institutions across the country. Tasked with transforming undergraduate music education to meet the needs of the 21st-century musician (Sarath et al., 2017), faculty members must come together to create a cohesive curriculum with a unified vision. We have tried to provide a balance of information in this text to support this endeavor.

For the researchers reading this text, we hope you will see it as catalyst for a new research agenda. Our work is grounded in research, but we often find ourselves relying on the work of those in general education. The questions that are fundamental to our work, questions about why music is important and how we stay relevant in a global society, are under-researched by our community. We have provided substantial information that can serve as a foundation for further research, and we hope we have provided a framework for future researchers to consider the important questions facing our profession.

We dedicated this edition of our book to the teachers who have persevered during one of the most stressful times in the history of public education. The Covid-19 pandemic has created an environment that is constantly shifting and changing and has resulted in an amplification of frustrated voices searching for answers in a time when there is no single answer. During one of our interviews, we asked a teacher, Steve, how he was doing. His answer speaks for many who have navigated their way through the past two years.

> I was walking out of school with one of our history teachers, and he looked at me and just said "So, how's it going?" I stopped and I looked at him and I said, "You know , to be honest I have no idea. I have no idea of what I did today. Was it the right thing to do for these kids? Because I don't know what needs to be done other than what I'm attempting to do right now, but I've never done this before, you know. Not having the regular feedback you get from just the facial expressions and all these other things. It's just so hard to figure out—is this the right thing to do or not?" And it was so funny, he just leaned back against the wall. He took a big breath in and let out a sigh and he said, "Well if you're feeling that way about it I guess it's okay that the rest of us are feeling that way about it." This is first-year teaching again for all of us … We are all trying to figure this thing out and at the end of the day all you can say is I gave it my best effort.

We have heard over the past several years, that many teachers interested in adopting a culturally responsive approach in their teaching are apprehensive, they are afraid of making mistakes and/or they are overwhelmed with what may seem like a complete overhaul of their curriculum. However, we encourage teachers not to allow their apprehensions to prevent them from taking any action at all. We are reminded of a quote often attributed to the late poet, writer, and civil rights activist Maya Angelou, who said, "I did then what I knew how to do. Now that I know better, I do better."

We often describe how change is hard, but change happens every day. The reality is that music education is changing and will continue to change. Our hope is that this change will intentionally be focused on culturally responsive pedagogy. As Allen, the high school band director, stated in response to the question of why culturally responsive teaching in music is important:

> It's because it's best educational practice. It is how we reach all of our students … All we have to do is look at the changing demographics of the United States to

realize that culturally responsive teaching is going to become more and more important instead of less important. It's just good teaching.

It is appropriate and significant that Allen's statement ends with a phrase that harks back to Gloria Ladson-Billings' landmark 1995 article making the case for culturally relevant pedagogy. We agree that culturally responsive teaching is effective educational practice, and it is becoming more important as we work to design a system from the ground up that is focused on the skills and needs of the 21st-century musician. In so many ways, culturally responsive teaching *is* "good teaching," but good teaching does not just happen. Good teaching is the result of hard work, dedication, and perseverance. It requires the best that we have to offer—but then, our future generations of musicians, both amateur and professional, deserve no less than our very best.

References

Baldwin, J. (1962, January 14). As much truth as one can bear [book review]. *The New York Times*, p. BR11.

Bledsoe, R. N. (2015). Music education for all? *The Music Educators Journal*, *28*(2), 18–22.

Ladson-Billings, G. (1995). But that's just good teaching! The case for culturally relevant pedagogy. *Theory into Practice, 34*, 159–165.

McKoy, C. L., Butler, A., & Lind, V. R. (2009). Conceptually framing music teaching and learning within the context of culture: Implications for music teacher education. In M. Schmidt (Ed.), *Collaborative action for change: Selected proceedings from the 2007 Symposium on Music Teacher Education* (pp. 51–70). Rowman & Littlefield.

National Association of Schools of Music. (2021). *Handbook: 2020–21*. Author. https://nasm.arts-accredit.org/wp-content/uploads/sites/2/2021/01/M-2020-21-Handbook-Final-01-08-2021.pdf

National Coalition for Core Arts Standards. (2014). *National core arts standards*. State Education Agency Directors of Arts Education. Available from www.nationalartsstandards.org/

National Endowment for the Arts (2011). Three NEA monographs on arts participation: A research digest. *NEA research note 101*. Author.

Regelski, T. (2007). Amateuring in music and its rivals. *Action, Criticism, and Theory for Music Education*, *6*(3), 22–50. http://act.maydaygroup.org/articles/Regelski6_3.pdf

Sarath, E. W., Myers, D. E., & Campbell, P. S. (2017). *Redefining music studies in an age of change: Creativity, diversity, and integration*. Routledge.

Small, C. (1998). *Musicking: The meanings of performing and listening*. Wesleyan University Press.

Villegas, A. M., & Lucas, T. (2002). Preparing culturally responsive teachers: Rethinking the curriculum. *Journal of Teacher Education*, *53*(1), 20–32. https://doi.org/10.1177/0022487102053001003

Wiggins, J. (2015). *Teaching for musical understanding*. Oxford University Press.

GLOSSARY OF TERMS

Asset-based pedagogy Pedagogy that values and builds upon the unique backgrounds, experiences, and funds of knowledge individual students bring to the classroom. It is a response to deficit-based pedagogies that view students who don't reflect "mainstream" ways of knowing and learning as being deficient.

Critical race theory (CRT) A theoretical framework developed in the 1970s and primarily attributed to Derrick Bell. It is an extension of critical legal studies and examines the role of U.S. law in perpetuating racism, which is viewed as a social construct rather than a biological characteristic. CRT also holds that racism is a result of complex and subtle social and institutional dynamics, rather than explicit and intentional prejudices of individuals. Concepts of CRT have been used as a framework for examining how racism functions in a variety of systems, including educational systems.

Cultural competence Originating in the field of health care, it is the ability to understand, appreciate, and interact with people from cultures or belief systems different from one's own. It is also one of the three pillars of Ladson-Billings' theory of culturally relevant pedagogy and refers to the ability to help students appreciate and celebrate their cultures of origin while gaining knowledge of and fluency in at least one other culture (Ladson-Billings, 2014).

Culturally relevant pedagogy A theoretical framework developed by Gloria Ladson-Billings (1995) that contradicts deficit-based pedagogies and seeks to influence teachers' attitudes and dispositions about working with culturally diverse student populations. The framework is comprised of three pillars or tenets: (1) academic success (teachers insist on academic excellence from their students), (2) cultural competence (teachers enable students to maintain their cultural integrity by using students' culture as a vehicle for learning), and

(3) critical consciousness (teachers enable students to critique cultural norms, values, and institutions that sustain social inequities).

Culturally responsive teaching According to Geneva Gay (2002), culturally responsive teaching uses the cultural characteristics, experiences, and perspectives of ethnically diverse students as conduits for teaching them more effectively. It teaches to and through students' strengths. It differs from culturally relevant pedagogy in that it prioritizes the development of competencies and methods that illustrate what culturally responsive teaching should look like in the classroom.

Culturally sustaining pedagogy (CSP) Formulated by Django Paris (2012) to address the superficial ways in which asset-based pedagogies such as culturally relevant pedagogy and culturally responsive teaching have been implemented in educational practice. It seeks to perpetuate and foster—to sustain—linguistic, literate, and cultural pluralism as part of schooling for positive social transformation and revitalization.

Multicultural education Refers to any form of education or teaching that incorporates the histories, texts, values, beliefs, and perspectives of people from different cultural backgrounds. At the classroom level, for example, teachers may modify or incorporate lessons to reflect the cultural diversity of the students in a particular class. In many cases, "culture" is defined in the broadest possible sense, encompassing race, ethnicity, nationality, language, religion, class, gender, sexual orientation, and "exceptionality"—a term applied to students with specialized needs or disabilities (*Glossary of Education Reform*, 2014).

Multicultural music education The most frequently used of several terms referring to the intersection of multicultural education, music education, and ethnomusicology. It involves teaching music in diverse cultures as well as teaching students of diverse cultural backgrounds (Campbell, 2018). It is related to but not synonymous with the study of world musics as multicultural music education examines the cultural aspects of music-making along with the unique musical elements that define a specific genre or type of music.

Social justice pedagogy The concept of social justice pedagogy is very similar to critical consciousness, the third tenet of Ladson-Billings' theoretical framework for culturally relevant pedagogy. Its objective is to develop students' awareness of injustices within societal structures that negatively and disproportionally impact groups historically marginalized by race, class, gender, attractional orientation, and ability while also providing students with the tools to dismantle them.

GLOSSARY REFERENCES

Campbell, P. S. (2018). *Music, education, and diversity: Bridging cultures and communities.* Teachers College Press.

Gay, G. (2002). Preparing for culturally responsive teaching. *Journal of Teacher Education, 53*(2), 106–116. https://doi.org/10.1177/0022487102053002003

Glossary of Education Reform. (2014). Multicultural education. In *Glossary of education reform.* www.edglossary.org/multicultural-education/

Ladson-Billings, G. (1995). Toward a theory of culturally relevant pedagogy. *American Educational Research Journal, 32*(3), 465–492.

Ladson-Billings, G. (2014). Culturally relevant pedagogy 2.0: AKA the remix. *Harvard Educational Review, 84*(1), 74–84.

Paris, D. (2012). Culturally sustaining pedagogy: A needed change in stance, terminology, and practice. *Educational Researcher, 41*(3), 93–97.

INDEX

Note: Page numbers in *italics* indicate figures.

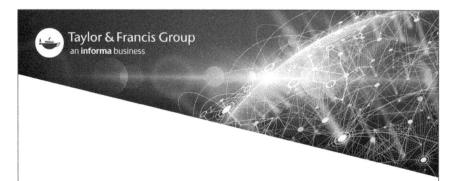

Lightning Source UK Ltd.
Milton Keynes UK
UKHW022118271222
414250UK00032B/949